THE CELL

Words in *italic* in the main text (*or in* Roman *type in the captions*) are explained in the Index and glossary at the end of the book.

A Cherrytree Book

Adapted by A S Publishing
from La Céllula, el origen de la vida
by Núria Roca and Marta Serrano
edited by Mercè Seix
illustrated by Antonio Muñoz Tenllado
designed by Rosa Mª Moreno
produced by Rafael Marfil

This edition first published 1996
by Cherrytree Press Ltd
a subsidiary of
The Chivers Company Ltd
Windsor Bridge Road
Bath, Avon BA2 3AX

British Library Cataloguing in Publication Data

The cell. – (Invisible world)
1. Cells – Juvenile literature 2. Cytology – Juvenile literature
I. Halton, Frances
611'.0181

ISBN 0-7451-5280-5

Typeset by Dorchester Typesetting Group Ltd. Dorset
Printed in Spain

INVISIBLE WORLD

THE CELL

Edited by
Frances Halton

CHERRYTREE BOOKS

The first cells

Every living thing is made of cells. Some, such as *bacteria* and *amoebas*, have only one cell; others have many millions. A cell itself is a living thing; it breathes, feeds, produces energy, grows and reproduces itself.

An adult human being is made up of more than 10 million million cells, so small that we can only see them by looking through a microscope. The size and shape of a cell depends on its function. Cells are all designed to carry out a specific job, for example to support our bodies, to move us around, to pass messages, and to make all the different substances our bodies need. They can also make new cells, for many of the cells in our bodies have only a short life and must be replaced when they wear out or die.

The first living things were single cells. How did they come into being? When our planet was formed 4600 million years ago, from clouds of gas and dust particles which circled the sun, its interior was molten, and it gave off gases including water vapour. These made up the earth's atmosphere. Gradually the planet cooled, and the water vapour turned into torrential rains that created the oceans. In them the first living things developed. Without water life, as we know it, cannot exist. This is how we know that our sort of life does not exist on other, waterless, planets.

Earlier this century a Russian biochemist called Alexander Ivanovich Oparin tried to explain how life came about. His theory was that the chemicals in the planet's atmosphere joined of their own accord to form simple *organic compounds – molecules* containing *carbon, oxygen, hydrogen* and *nitrogen.* These organic molecules fell into the oceans over long periods of time, and created what Oparin called the primeval soup. In the soup the molecules linked together to form even more complex molecules. Eventually they acquired the basic characteristics of a living thing; the first cells had appeared.

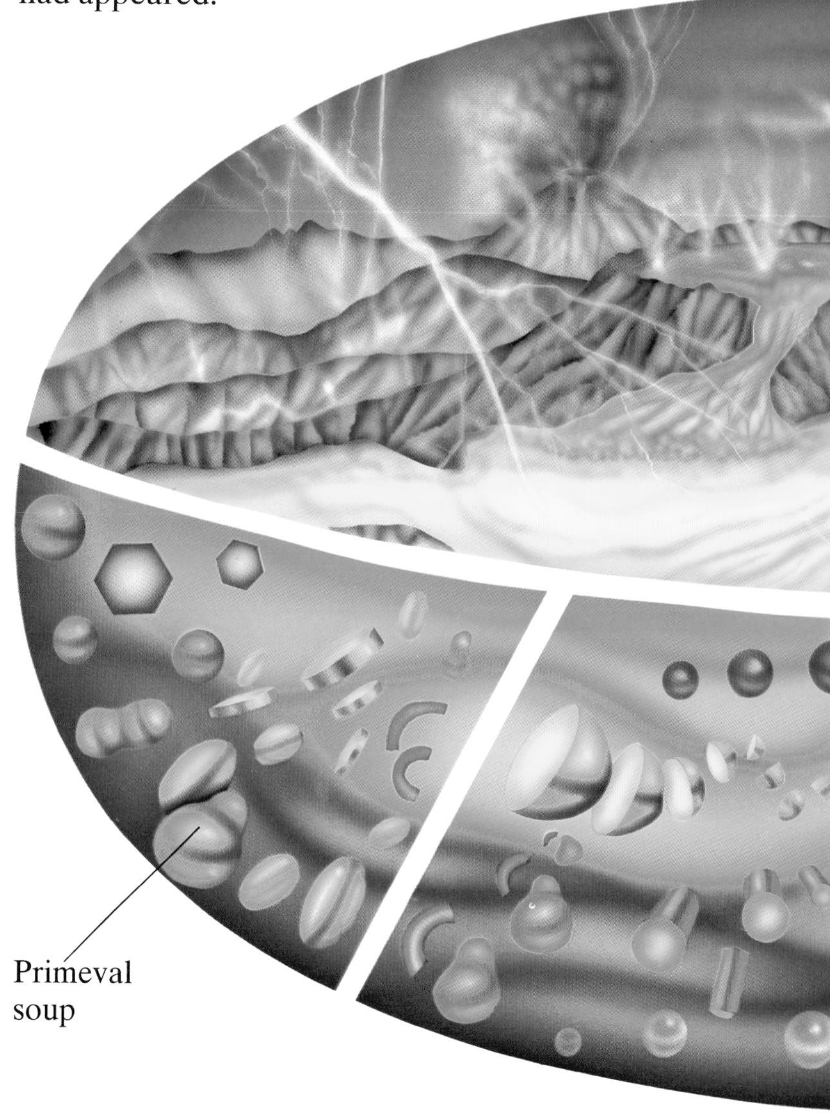

Primeval soup

Lightning and heat from the earth's volcanic surface caused chemicals in the atmosphere to form compounds. Some of these were organic molecules, which over millions of years linked together. They formed the forerunners of proteins *and* nucleic acids, *the essential molecules on which life forms are based.* ▼

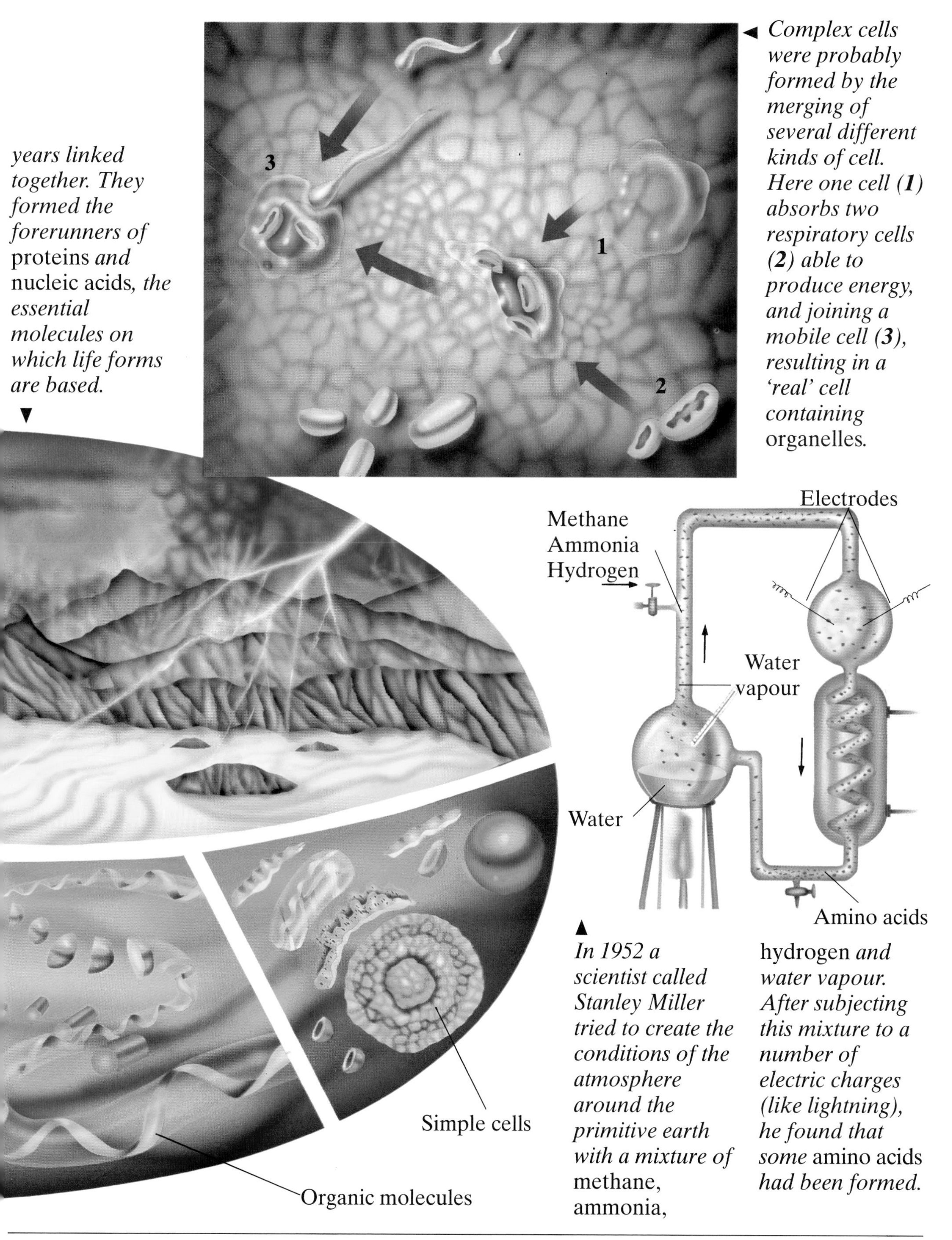

◀ *Complex cells were probably formed by the merging of several different kinds of cell. Here one cell (**1**) absorbs two respiratory cells (**2**) able to produce energy, and joining a mobile cell (**3**), resulting in a 'real' cell containing* organelles.

▲ *In 1952 a scientist called Stanley Miller tried to create the conditions of the atmosphere around the primitive earth with a mixture of* methane, ammonia, hydrogen *and* water vapour. *After subjecting this mixture to a number of electric charges (like lightning), he found that some* amino acids *had been formed.*

Living molecules

All living things, including animals and plants, are made up largely of organic molecules. These molecules are compounds of the four chemical elements carbon, oxygen, hydrogen and nitrogen; among the molecules formed by them are *carbohydrates, lipids* (fats), proteins and nucleic acids. As well as these organic compounds, living things contain large amounts of water, and other inorganic molecules such as compounds of calcium and phosphorus.

Carbohydrates include starches and sugars. These are broken down into *glucose*, and used in the cells as fuel to produce energy, or stored there in the form of *glycogen*.

Lipids also act as fuel for the cell, and help to make up its outer covering, or *membrane*. They include a large number of compounds, which are almost insoluble in water.

Proteins are the main 'building materials' of our bodies and they play a key part in almost all the processes of life. They are found in many foods. They are broken down by *digestion* into units called amino acids. In the cells these are used to make up new proteins. Some of these proteins are used for growth or for the repair of damaged areas. Others are used to keep our bodies working.

Nucleic acids are the most complex organic molecules in the cell. They are made up of smaller units called chemical bases. There are two types of nucleic acid: deoxyribonucleic acid (*DNA*) and ribonucleic acid (*RNA*). The molecules of DNA contain coded instructions for every action of every cell in your body, in sections called *genes*. We inherit our DNA from our parents, and it is also referred to as genetic, or hereditary, material. The molecules of DNA are arranged in a double helix, or spiral. RNA makes copies of the coded instructions on the DNA, and takes these to the different parts of the cell.

A model (bottom) and a diagram of a DNA molecule. The molecule has the form of a double helix: it is made up of two chains of chemical units called bases, which are coiled parallel to each other to create a structure similar to a spiral staircase. The two chains are kept in position by links formed between their bases.

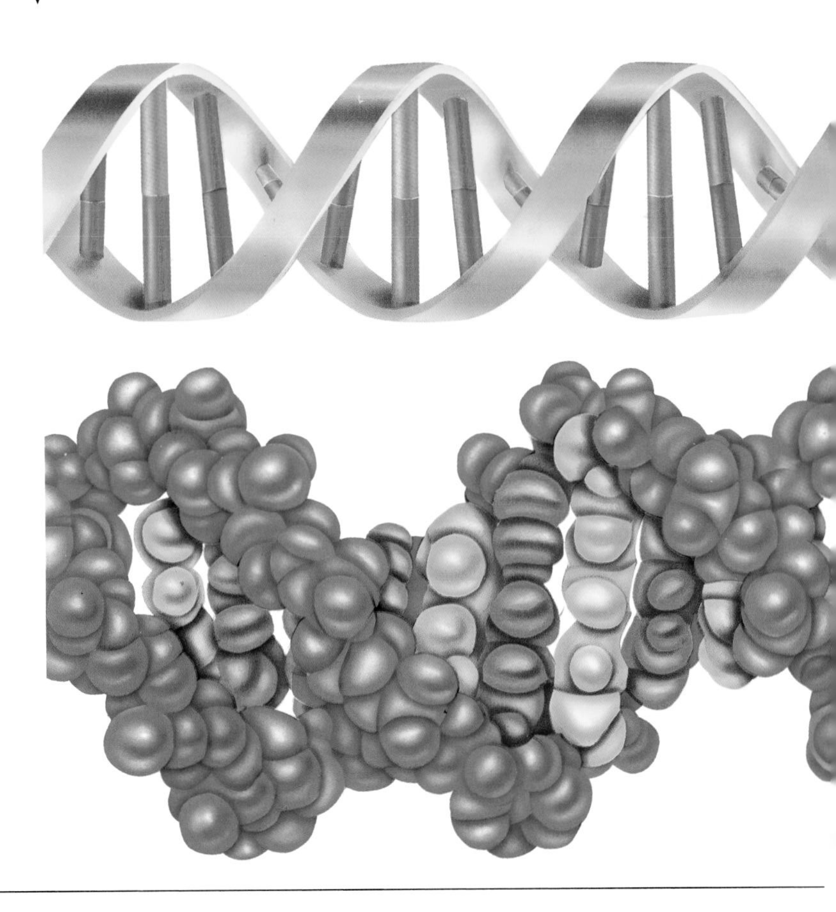

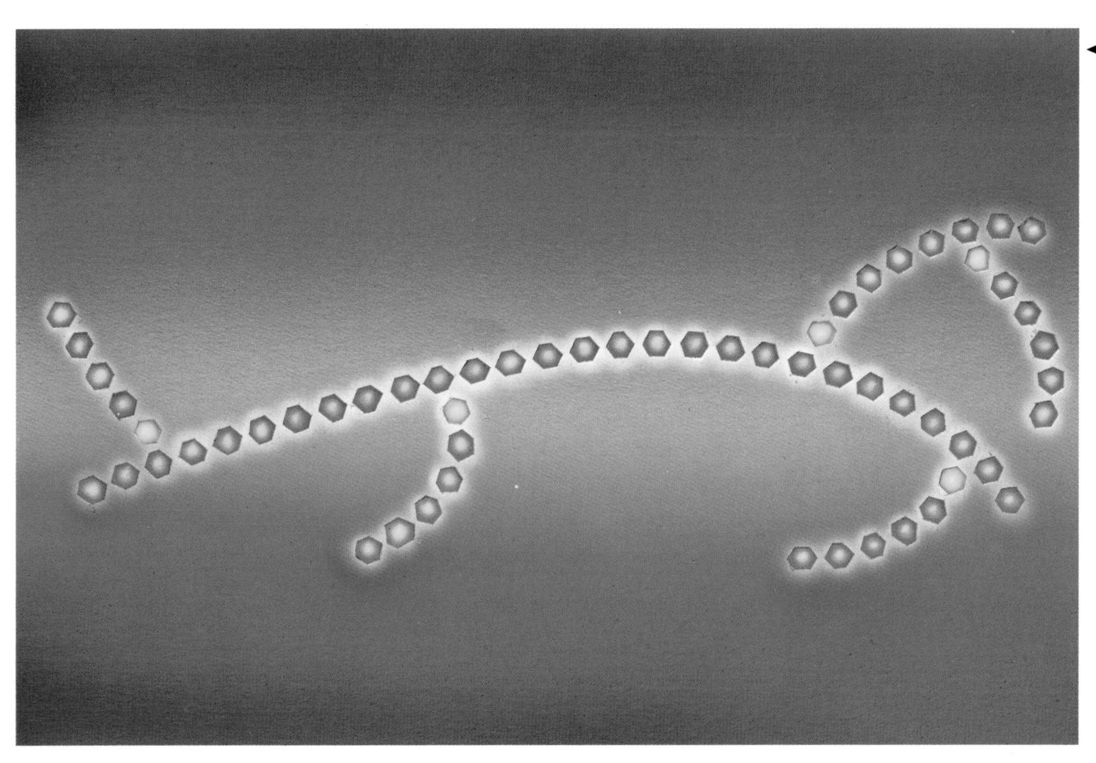

◄ *Living things need a continuous supply of energy. One of the forms in which they store it is glycogen, a long chain of glucose molecules. When energy is needed, this chain is broken down and the glucose molecules are released for use.*

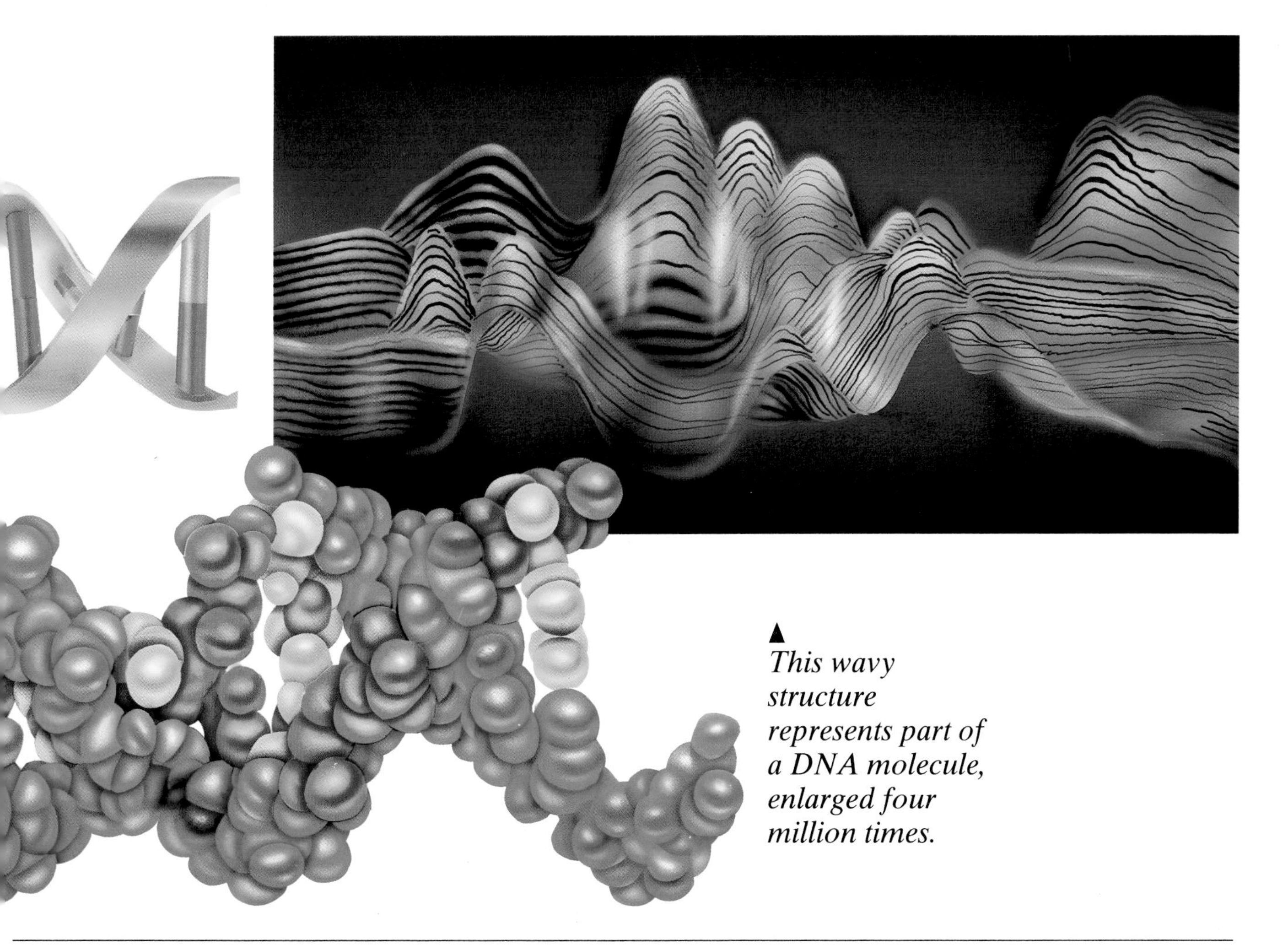

▲ *This wavy structure represents part of a DNA molecule, enlarged four million times.*

Inside the cell

Many different kinds of cell go to make up living things, but they all share some basic characteristics. Most living cells, including nearly all those that make up the human body, have three main parts: the cell membrane (sometimes called the plasma membrane), the *cytoplasm* and the *nucleus*.

The cell membrane is the outer covering of the cell, completely enclosing it. The membrane is semi-permeable, which means that it allows some substances to pass through it. It is made of a double layer of lipids, in which are embedded proteins. *Receptor molecules* in the membrane respond to external signals and substances, and set off actions within the cell.

The cytoplasm is a watery liquid containing useful substances such as *nutrients* and structures called organelles. These carry out specific functions, and include ribosomes, the endoplasmic reticulum, the Golgi apparatus, lysosomes and mitochondria.

Ribosomes are the cell's protein manufacturing units. They are globular particles that float about in the cytoplasm or are attached to the walls of the endoplasmic reticulum. This is a continuous network of membranes and channels. The proteins formed in the ribosomes move around the cell through these channels.

The Golgi apparatus is made of piles of tiny, disc-shaped sacs containing substances made in the cell, which will be needed in other parts of the body, for example the chemicals called *hormones*. Lysosomes contain special proteins called *enzymes*, which break down other substances such as bacteria.

The mitochondria are the cell's powerhouses, where oxygen and nutrients such as glucose are converted into the energy the cell needs to carry out all its functions.

The complex processes that take place in the cell, transforming substances into energy and useful products, and getting rid of waste products, are together known as *metabolism*.

The nucleus is the control centre of the cell. It is surrounded by its own membrane, and contains long threads of DNA made up of sections called genes. The genes carry the coded instructions for all the functions of our bodies. The nucleus also contains RNA which makes copies of the genes and takes them to the organelles.

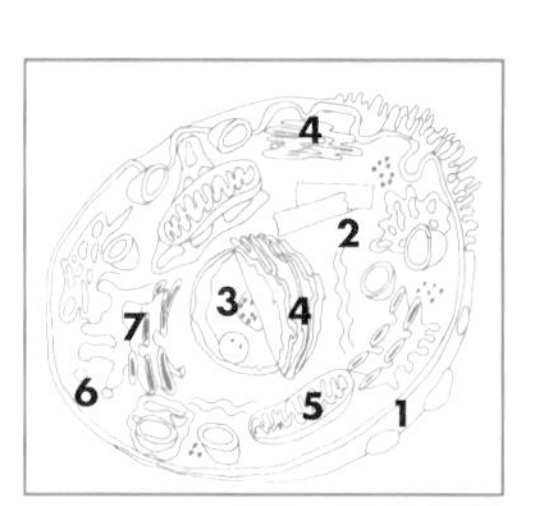

*The cells of the human body, like those of almost all living things, have three main parts: the cell membrane (**1**), the cytoplasm (**2**) and the nucleus (**3**). In the cytoplasm are structures called organelles which include the endoplasmic reticulum (**4**), mitochondria (**5**), lysosomes (**6**) and the Golgi apparatus (**7**).* ►

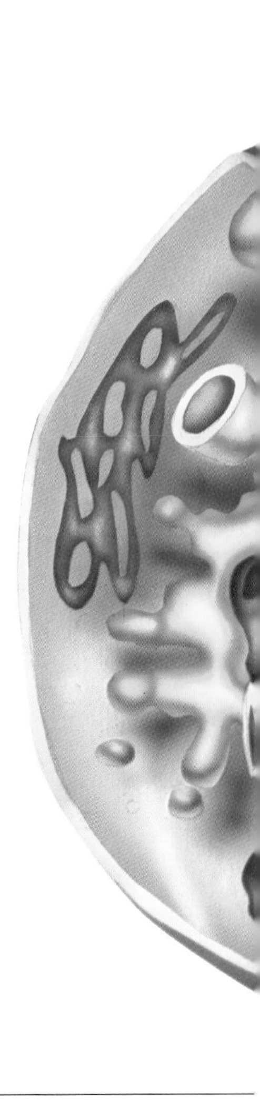

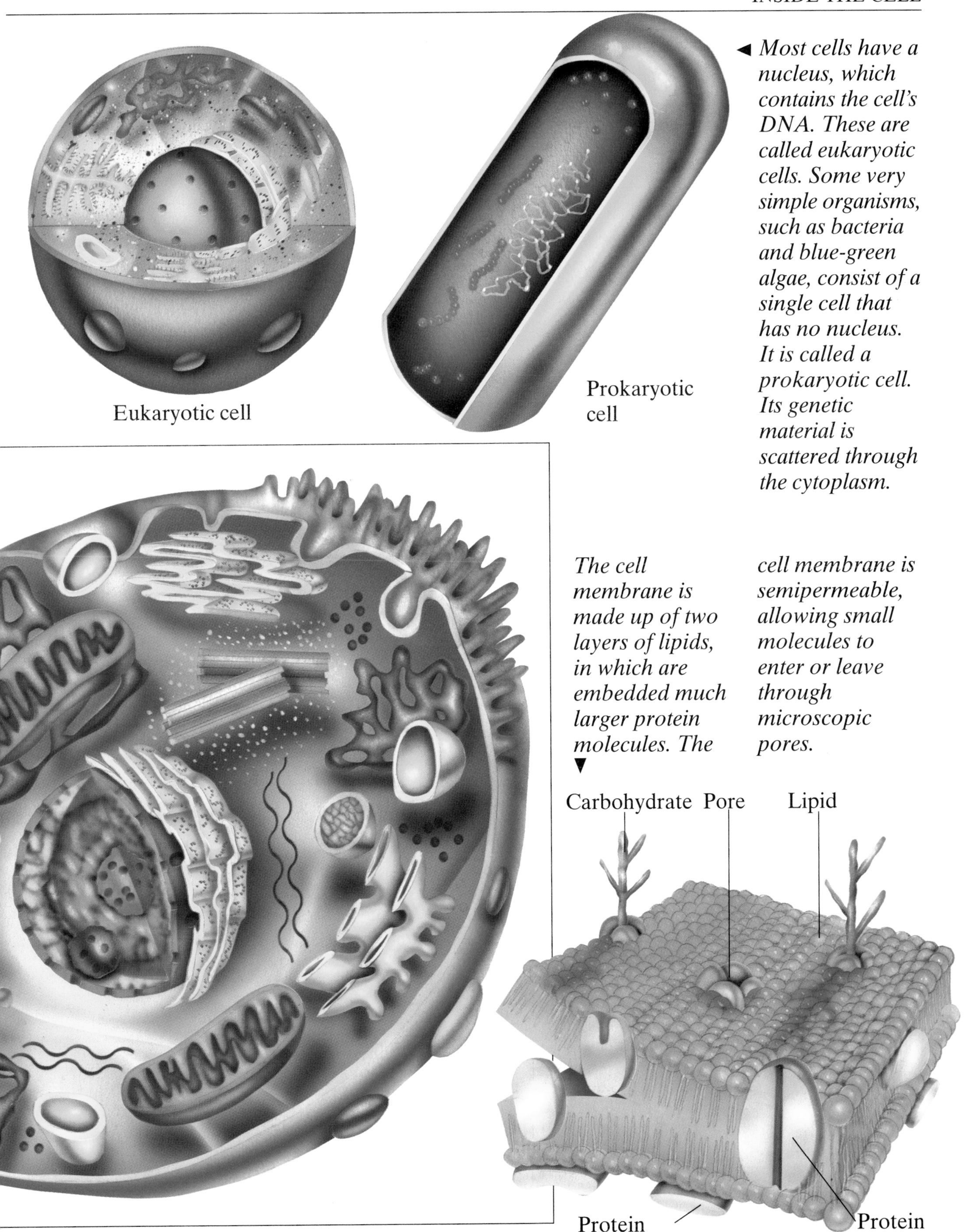

◄ *Most cells have a nucleus, which contains the cell's DNA. These are called eukaryotic cells. Some very simple organisms, such as bacteria and blue-green algae, consist of a single cell that has no nucleus. It is called a prokaryotic cell. Its genetic material is scattered through the cytoplasm.*

The cell membrane is made up of two layers of lipids, in which are embedded much larger protein molecules. The cell membrane is semipermeable, allowing small molecules to enter or leave through microscopic pores. ▼

Supplies for the cell

All cells, from the simplest to the most complicated, need regular supplies of energy and raw materials in order to live, to carry out their functions and to reproduce themselves. Supplies are carried to our cells by the blood. This contains nutrients obtained from our food through digestion, and oxygen from the air we breathe, which is picked up by the blood on its way through the lungs. The blood also collects substances made in our cells, such as hormones, and delivers them to cells in other parts of the body.

In order to get into the cell, these substances must pass through its outer membrane. Small particles or molecules from the bloodstream pass through the membrane without difficulty, but larger ones enter the cell through a process called *phagocytosis*. This process is important in many *invertebrate animals* and especially in single-celled organisms. In phagocytosis the particles are surrounded, or engulfed, by part of the cell membrane. This closes round them to create a small sac, or vesicle, which is then taken inside the cell where its contents are broken down. This is the process used by *white blood cells* to destroy bacteria or germs in our bodies.

Just the opposite happens in *exocytosis*, the process in which large molecules or undigested particles leave the cell. Granules containing these substances go to the inner cell wall. There their membranes merge with the cell membrane which opens and lets out the contents.

Once food materials are inside the cell, it starts to digest them further. Organelles called lysosomes, which contain digestive enzymes, act as the stomach of the cell. They merge with the vesicles around the ingested particles and break them down in a process called heterophagy. Lysosomes are also responsible for breaking down parts of the cell that need to be destroyed, for example old organelles which have to be replaced. This process of self-destruction is called autophagy. The products of the lysosomes' digestion pass into the cytoplasm; they will either be used in the building of new molecules and cellular structures, or will be broken down even more by the mitochondria to release energy to fuel the cell. These processes are called *anabolism* and *catabolism*.

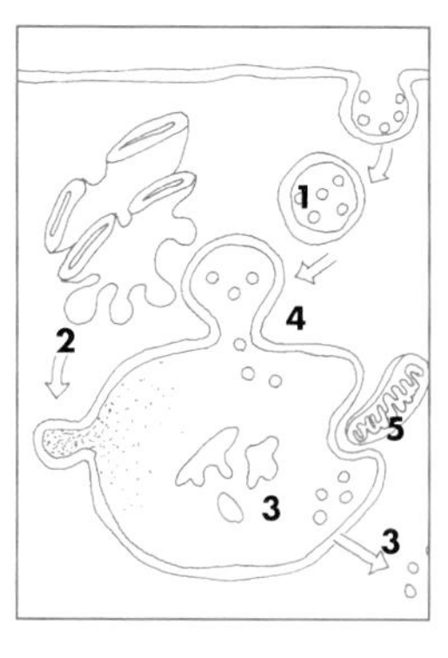

*The cell membrane closes round an invading substance to form a little sac called a vesicle (**1**). This is taken into the cell where it is surrounded by lysosomes (**2**), organelles that contain enzymes capable of breaking down complex molecules into simple molecules (**3**). This process is called heterophagy (**4**). In autophagy (**5**) the cell's own structures, such as old organelles, are broken down.* ▶

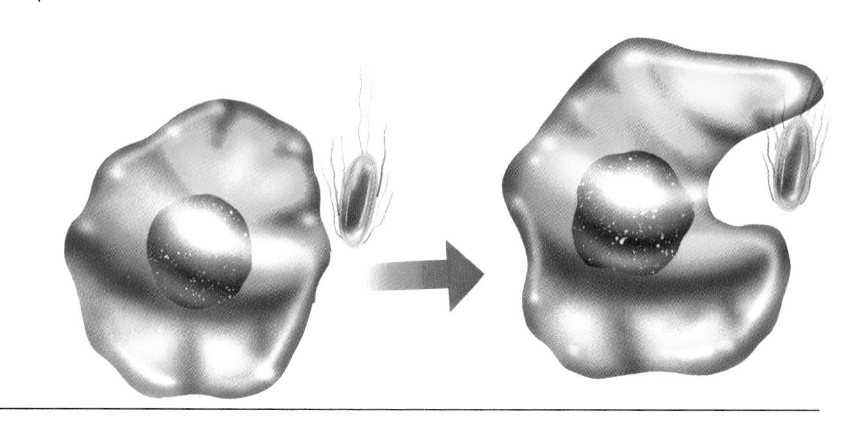

White blood cells called granulocytes and monocytes help to defend the body against harmful bacteria. ▼

In phagocytosis, they surround the bacteria, take them into the cell interior and break them down with enzymes.

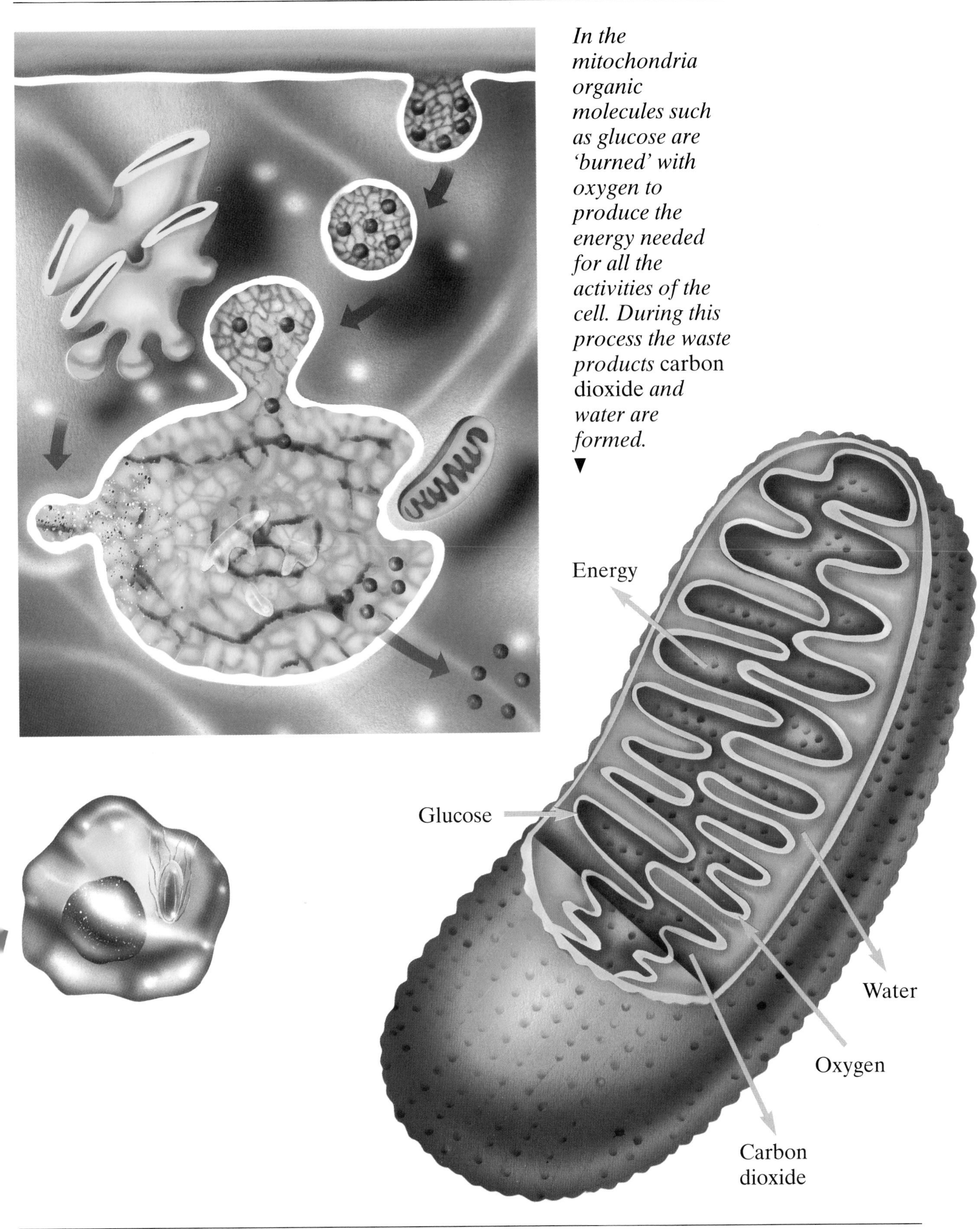

In the mitochondria organic molecules such as glucose are 'burned' with oxygen to produce the energy needed for all the activities of the cell. During this process the waste products carbon dioxide *and* water *are formed.* ▼

Cells in action

Cells continuously receive information from their environment and detect changes in it. Typical stimuli are chemical changes, changes in temperature and pressure, the presence of bacteria or foreign substances and so on. The cell membrane plays an important part in this sensitivity, as it contains many structures that detect stimuli.

Some of our cells are specially sensitive to physical and chemical stimuli. These are called receptor, or sensory, cells. They include cells in the skin that detect changes in temperature, and those of the sense organs that detect light, sound, smell and so on. They react to the stimuli by sending messages along nerve fibres to the *brain*.

One way in which cells respond to stimuli is by moving. Human body cells move in a number of different ways. Some white blood cells, which form part of the body's defence system, travel through the body to fight infections. They swim around in the blood with the help of little projections of their cytoplasm and cell membrane known as pseudopods, or false feet. When a foreign substance such as a bacterium enters the body, it makes substances called peptides at the site of the infection, and these peptides attract the white cells. When they reach the infecting organisms they destroy them by phagocytosis.

Male sex cells, called sperm or *spermatozoa*, have long tails called flagella, which lash to and fro to propel the spermatozoa through the female reproductive tract to the *ovum* (egg). Cells in the mucous membrane lining the respiratory tract have tiny hairlike projections called *cilia*. These are covered by a layer of sticky *mucus*, which traps particles of dust and other substances that are breathed in. By waving to and fro together, the cilia propel along the mucus and the particles trapped in it and expel them from the body.

The cells in some areas of the mucous membrane that lines the respiratory tract have tiny hairlike projections called cilia. In a waving motion, these sweep along the layer of mucus covering them, in which particles of dust and other harmful substances are trapped. ▼

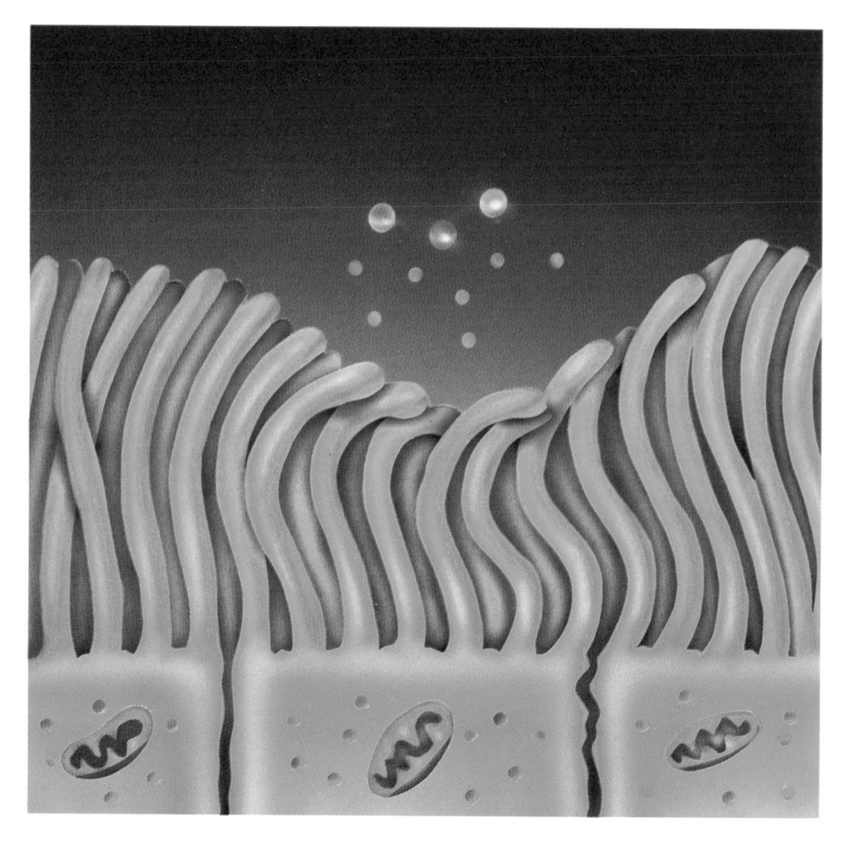

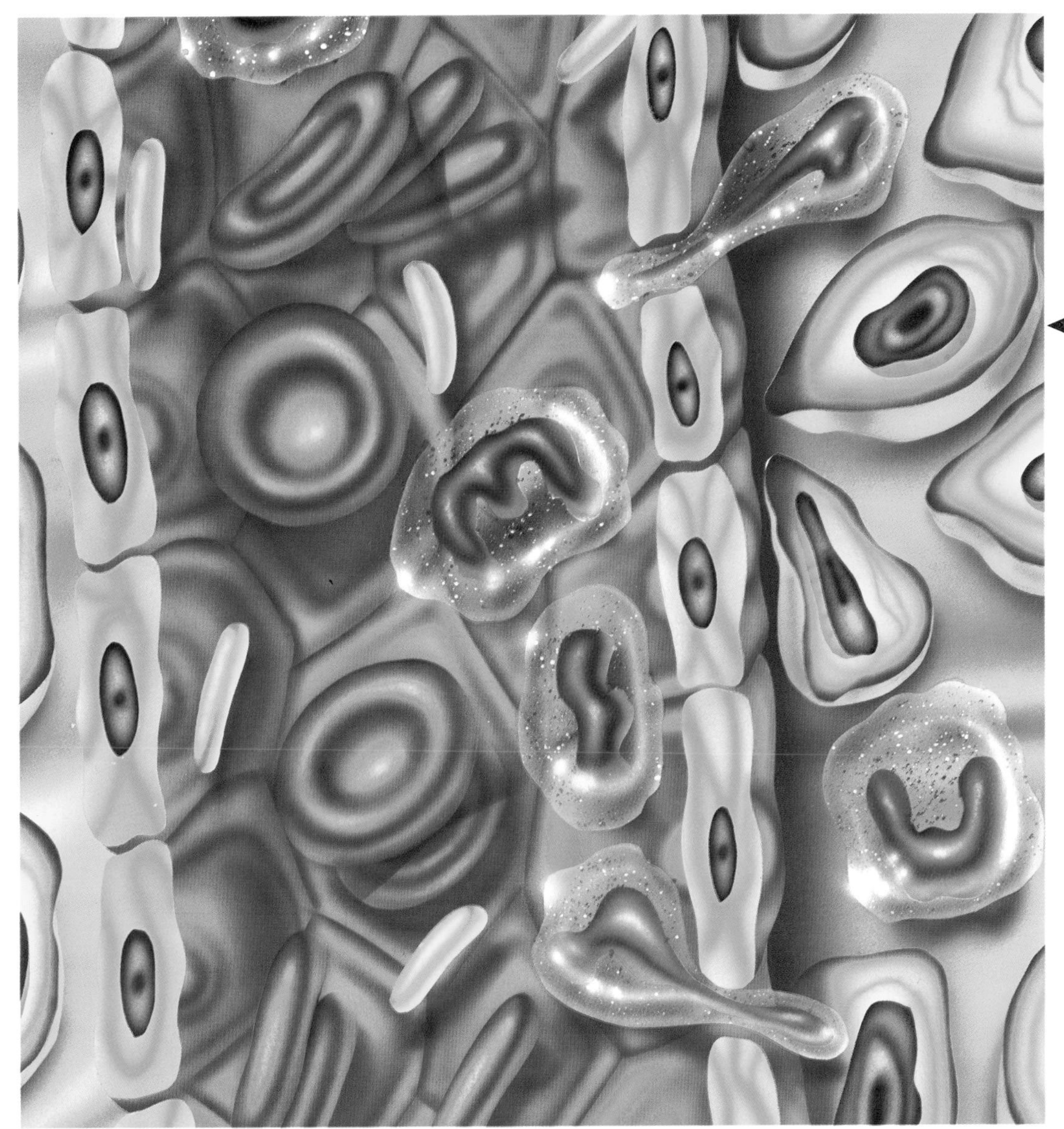

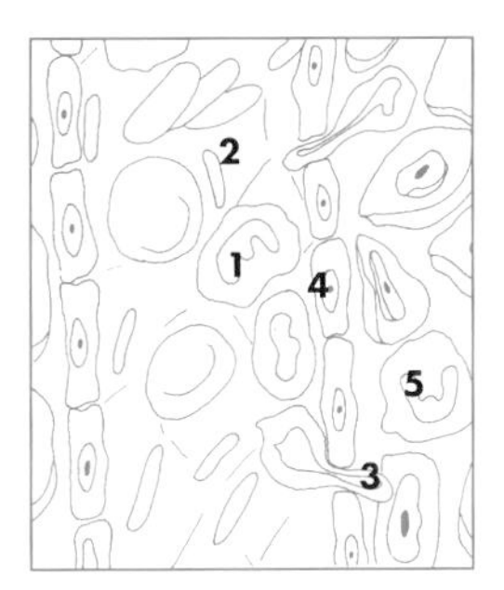

◄ *When part of the body is infected, substances are released that attract white blood cells (**1**) to the site. Once there, they make their way out of the* blood vessels *(**2**) by slipping projections called pseudopods (**3**) between the cells (**4**) of the wall. The white blood cells (**5**) engulf and destroy the invaders.*

Spermatozoa move at a speed of about four millimetres a minute as they make their way towards the ovum, propelled by their thrashing tail-like flagella. ▼

How cells reproduce

Like all living things, cells can reproduce. Most cells reproduce themselves by a process called *mitosis*. In this process a single parent cell divides to form two identical daughter cells. The genes, which control the way in which the cell will develop and function, are carried on threadlike structures called *chromosomes*. Before the cell divides, each chromosome copies, or duplicates, itself, forming two identical *chromatids*. The membrane round the nucleus breaks down, and structures called centrioles send out fibres that pull one chromatid from each pair to opposite sides of the cell. New nuclear membranes form round each group, and the cell divides into two daughter cells, each containing exactly the same genetic material as the parent cell.

Human beings all develop from a single cell, which is created by the joining up of an ovum from the mother and a sperm, or spermatozoon from the father. This cell quickly divides and each cell so formed divides again and again to build up our bodies. We grow because the number of cells in our body increases, and the larger we are, the more cells make up our body (the size of the individual cells stays the same).

Even when we have stopped growing some cells still go on making new cells, to replace those that have worn out. Among these are the cells that line the stomach and form the skin. Others, such as the cells that form bone, stop growing when we reach a certain age.

The ovum and sperm are known as sex cells. They are formed by a special type of cell division called *meiosis*, which takes place in a man's testicles and a woman's ovaries. Each sex cell has only half the number of chromosomes in the normal cells – in humans there are 23 chromosomes instead of 46. When the ovum and spermatozoon join they form a *zygote* containing 46 chromosomes, 23 from the mother and 23 from the father.

There are four stages in mitosis. In the prophase each chromosome copies itself to form identical chromatids. In the metaphase, the chromosomes move to the centre of the cell. In the anaphase one chromatid from each pair is drawn to opposite sides of the cell, and in the telophase new nuclear membranes form round each chromosome group and the cell divides.

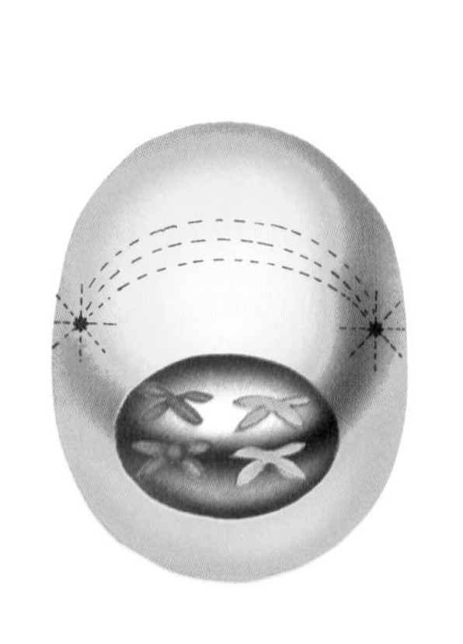

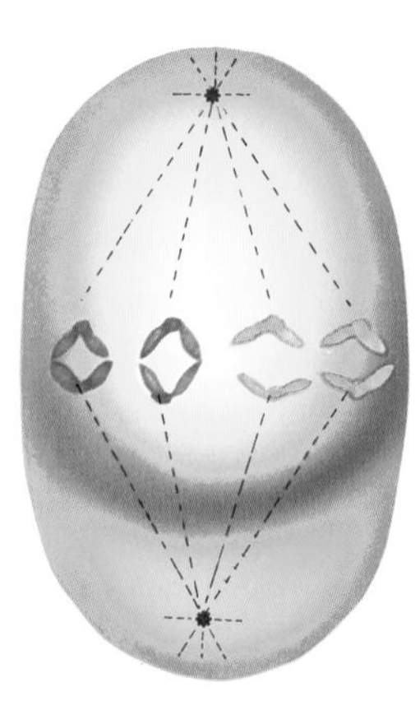

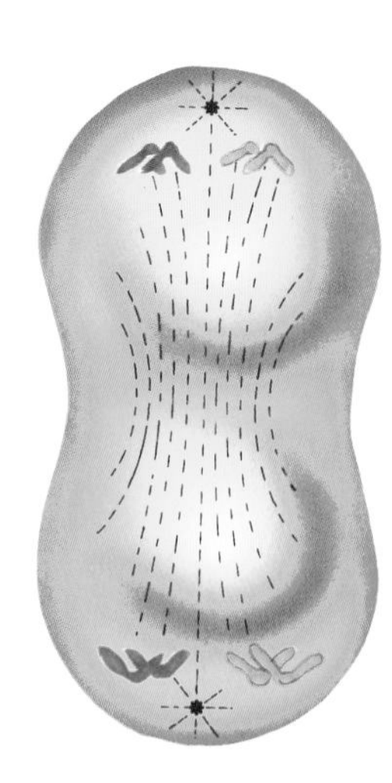

PROPHASE METAPHASE ANAPHASE

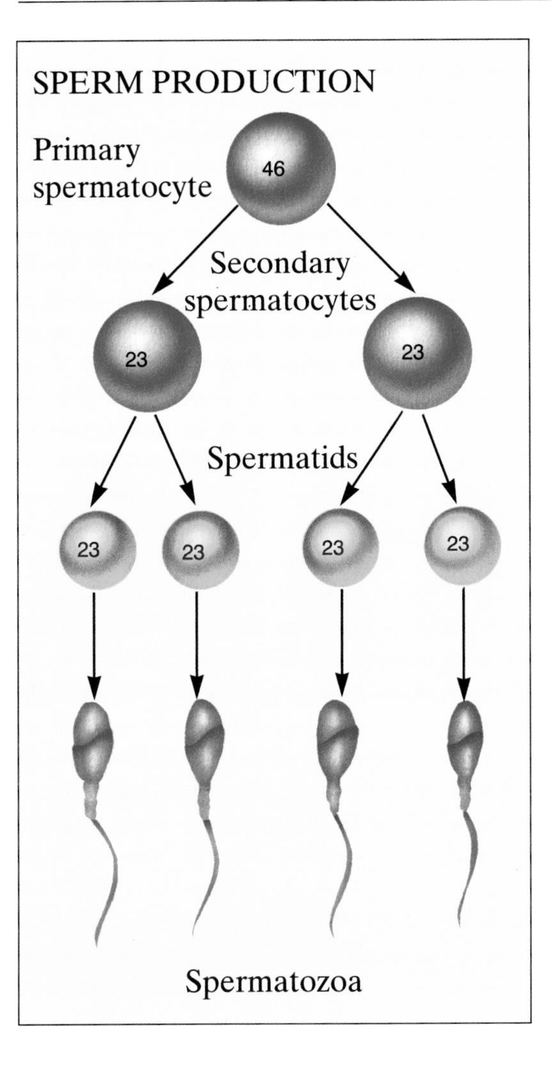

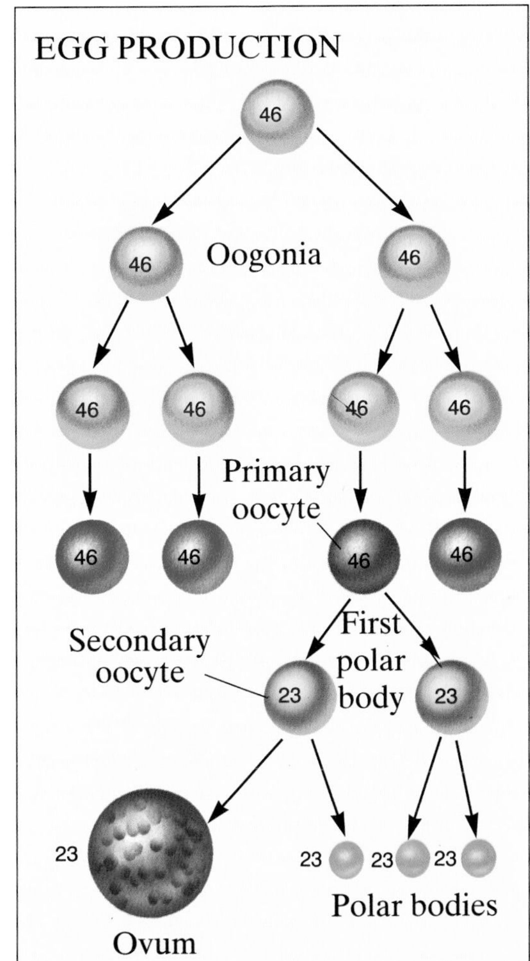

◄ *Sex cells are formed by meiosis, which consists of two separate divisions. Four sperm cells are created from each male primary spermatocyte, whereas only one egg, or ovum, results from each female primary oocyte division. The figures indicate the number of chromosomes present at each stage. The polar bodies play no further part in reproduction.*

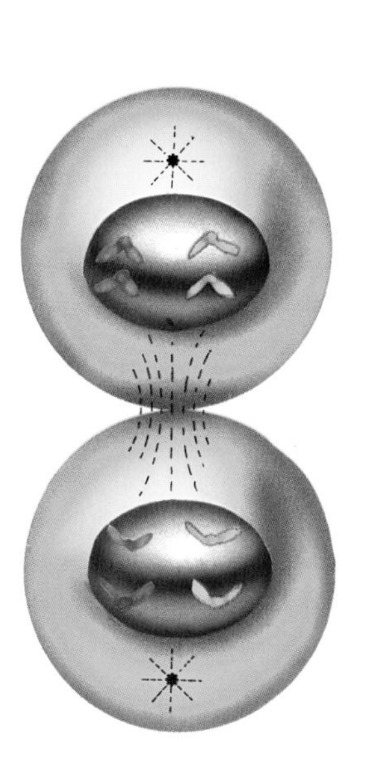

TELOPHASE

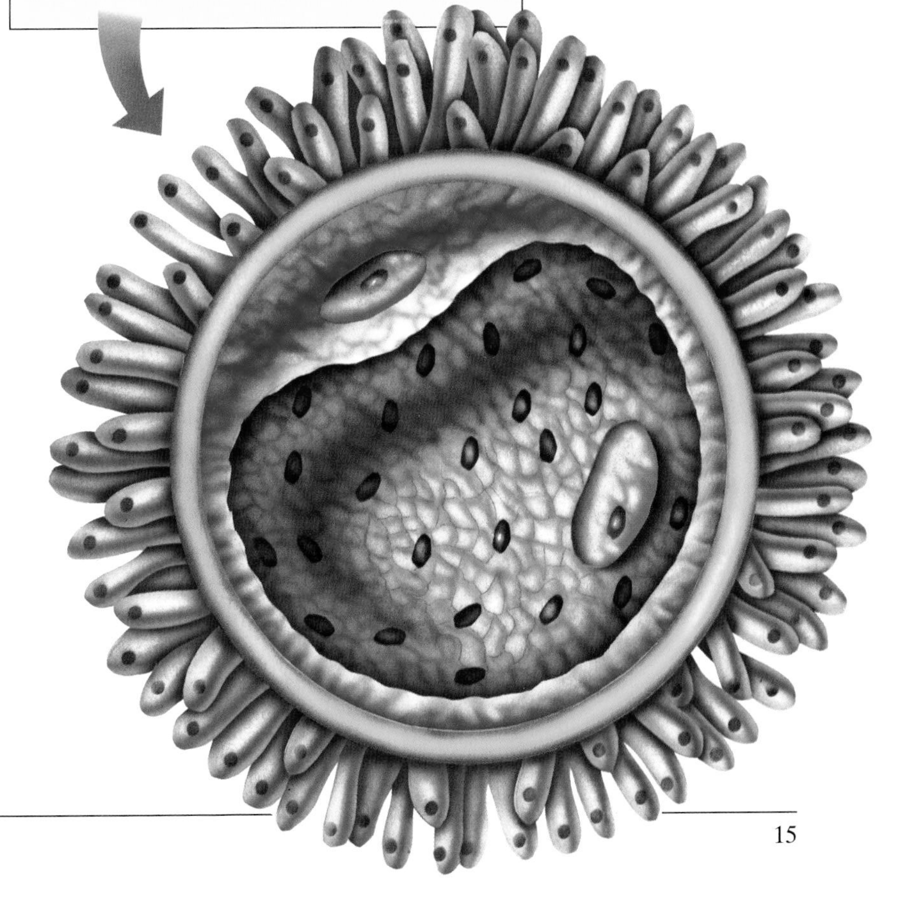

Cell design

Every cell in the human body is descended from a single cell, the zygote. But although all our cells come from this one cell, and all of them contain exactly the same genetic material, they are of many different shapes and sizes, and are specialized to carry out different functions. Some have fingerlike projections of the cell membrane called *microvilli*, which increase the surface area. Some have 'tails' to enable them to move. Some are over a metre long.

Our bodies have more than 200 different kinds of cell. The first few generations of cells coming from the original zygote are all identical. But at a certain point in the development of the *embryo* its cells begin to differentiate, or develop along different lines. Cells that carry out the same functions, and so have a similar shape and structure, cluster together to form *tissues*. Our bodies contain many different kinds of tissue: nerve tissue, muscle tissue, bone tissue and so on. Some tissues combine to form organs, such as the heart, the lungs, and the liver. The heart, for example, is made up of muscle tissue, *epithelial tissue* and nerve tissue.

Several organs can work together in a *system*. The respiratory system, for example, is concerned with taking in oxygen and expelling the waste product carbon dioxide; it is formed of a group of organs (the nose, pharynx, larynx, trachea, bronchi, and lungs) which are in turn composed of different types of tissue (epithelial, *cartilaginous, connective* and so on).

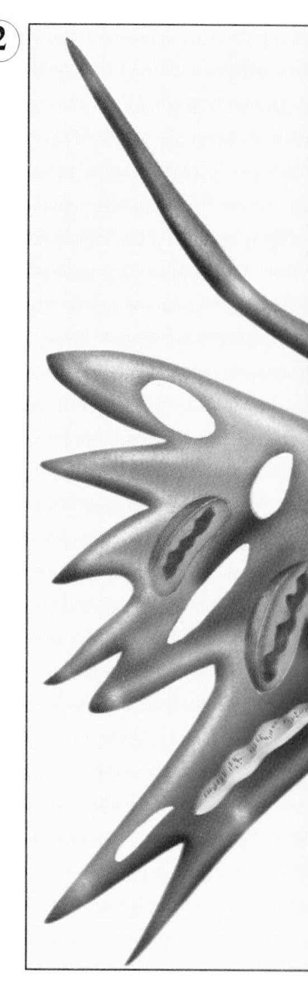

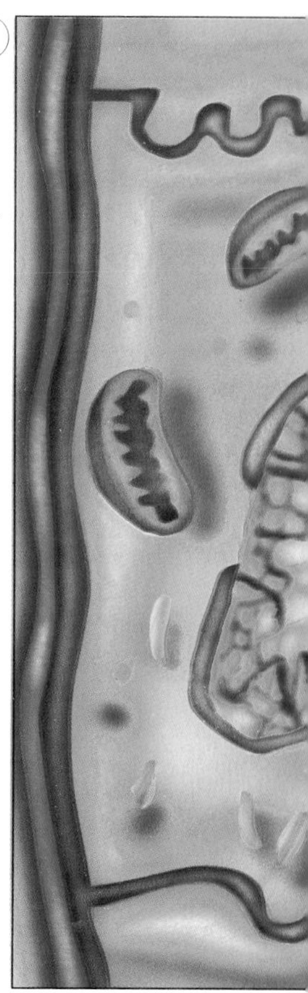

*Although all the cells in the human body have exactly the same genetic material in their nuclei, they develop in a number of different ways. Epithelial tissue covers and lines organs such as the stomach (**1**). The tissue makes mucus. This protects the cells from damage by digestive juices in the stomach. Connective tissue (**2**) fills the gaps between our organs. Cells in it, called fibroblasts, contain large numbers of ribosomes. These make the proteins needed to build up the collagen and elastin fibres with which the cells surround themselves.* ►

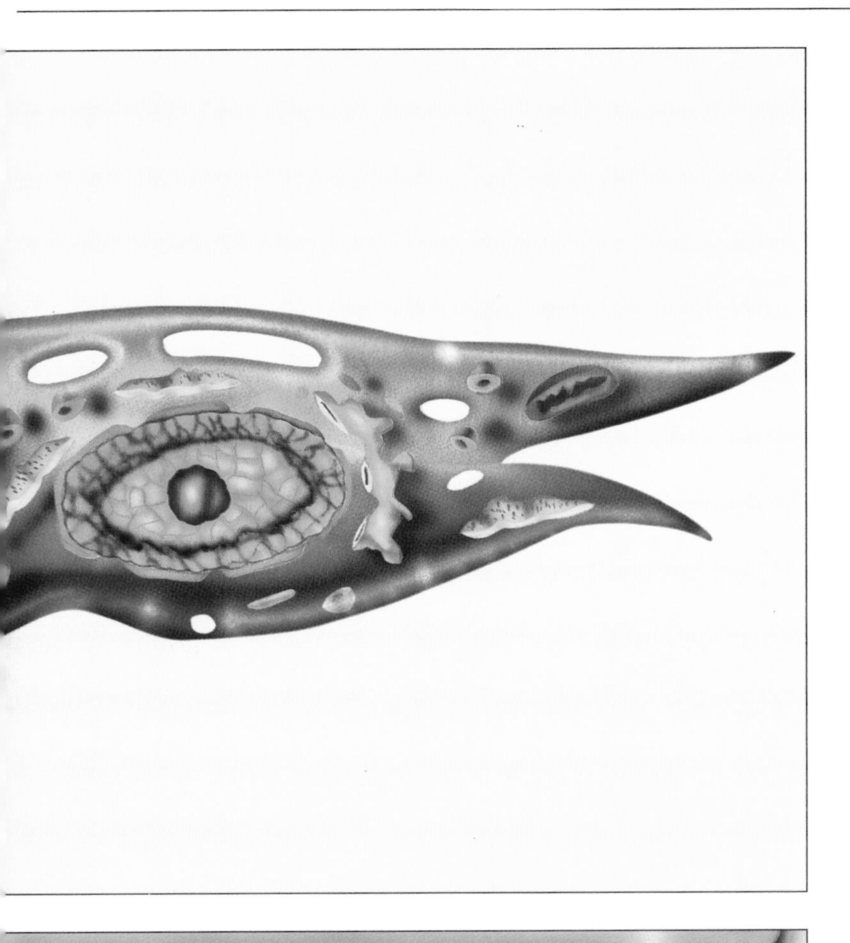

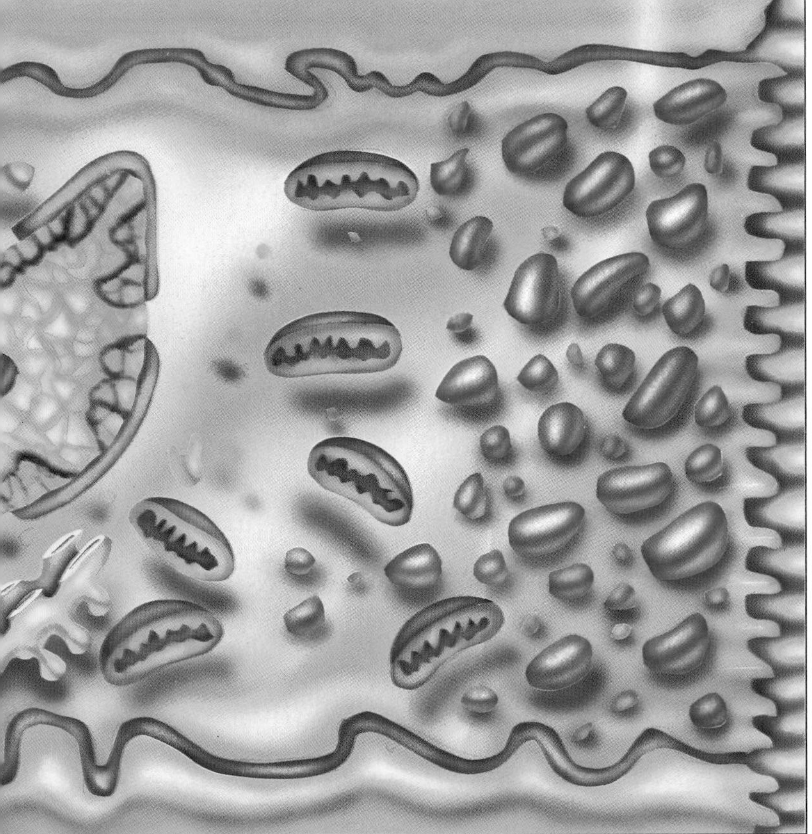

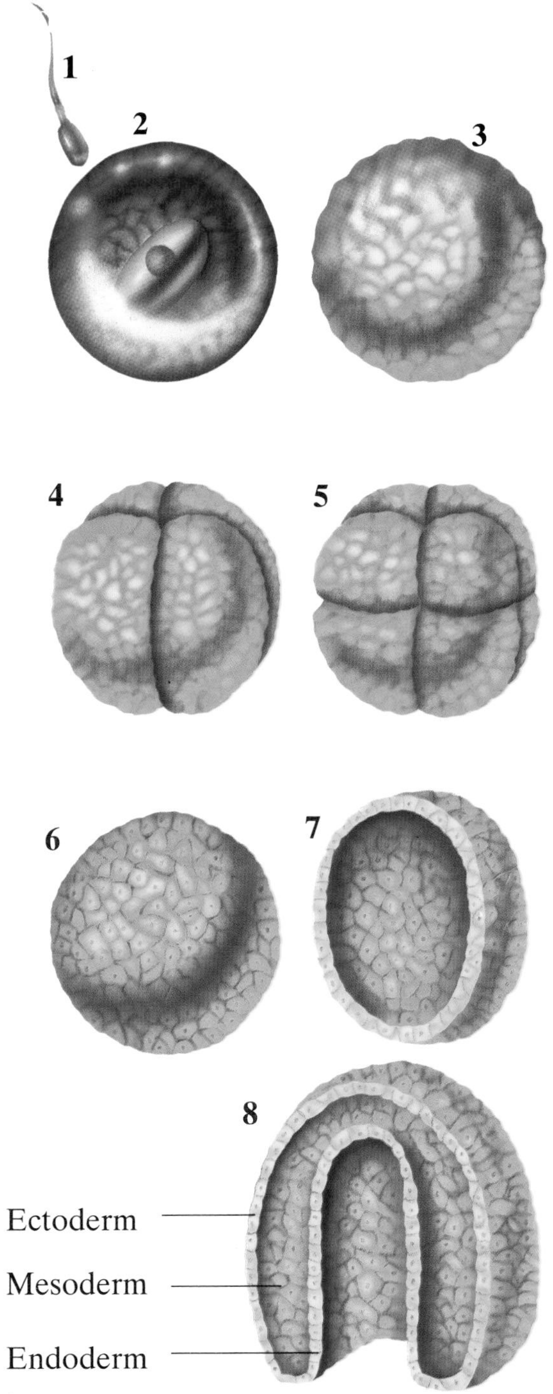

▲ *A sperm (**1**) joins an ovum (**2**) to form a zygote (**3**). It divides many times to form a solid cluster of identical cells called a morula (**4**, **5**), and then a hollow sphere called a blastula (**6**, **7**). In the next phase, gastrulation (**8**), three layers of cells are formed, and the cells now begin to develop differently.*

Bone cells

Our bodies are held together, kept in shape and supported by three types of tissue: connective, cartilaginous and bony. Connective tissue is made up of a small number of star-shaped cells called fibroblasts. They are surrounded by fibres of the proteins collagen and elastin, and all are embedded in a spongy material called the matrix. All this surrounding material is made by the fibroblasts, which can also repair it when necessary.

Connective tissue binds together and connects other tissues and organs. For example, it covers bundles of nerve and muscle fibres, forms a tough outer covering for the kidneys and holds them in place, and forms strong ligaments that connect bones and stretchy tendons that connect muscles and bones. In some places it contains adipose cells, the cytoplasm of which consists almost entirely of fat.

Cartilaginous tissue is tough, strong and rubbery. It is made of bulky, round cells called chondrocytes, surrounded by a stretchy substance. This sort of tissue makes up our ear lobes, epiglottis and part of the nose. Most of our bones begin as cartilage, but as we grow up the cartilage is replaced by fibrous tissue that hardens into bone in a process called ossification. This process is not completed until we are about 20 years old.

Bony tissue contains three types of cell: *osteoblasts, osteocytes* and *osteoclasts*, surrounded by a matrix of protein fibres and hard minerals, particularly calcium. Osteoblasts are responsible for forming the bony tissue. They have a cube- or prism-shaped cell body, from which extend little extensions of cytoplasm. Their cytoplasm has a large number of organelles that specialize in making the protein fibres and mineral molecules of the bony matrix. When an osteoblast has surrounded itself with bony tissue, it turns into an osteocyte. The cytoplasm of an osteocyte has the same organelles as an osteoblast, but fewer of them. The osteoclasts, which are quite round and large, are responsible for breaking down bone.

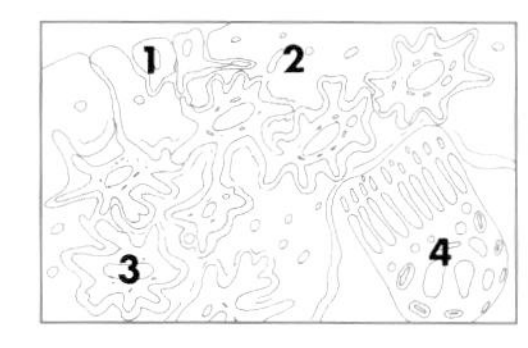

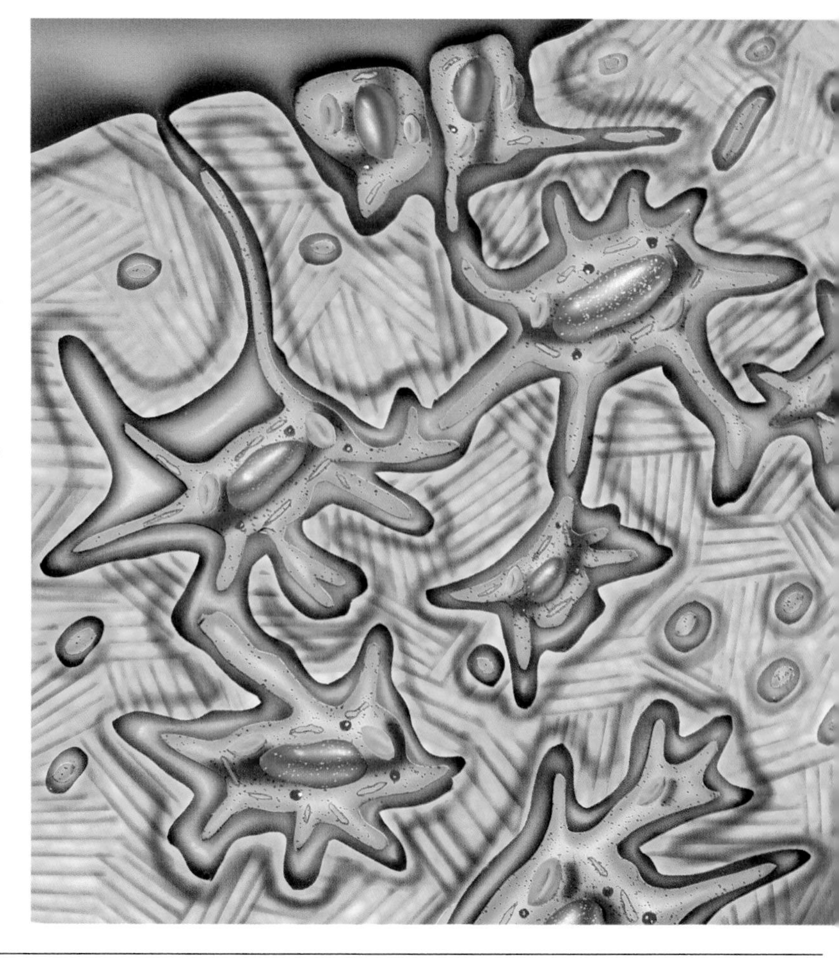

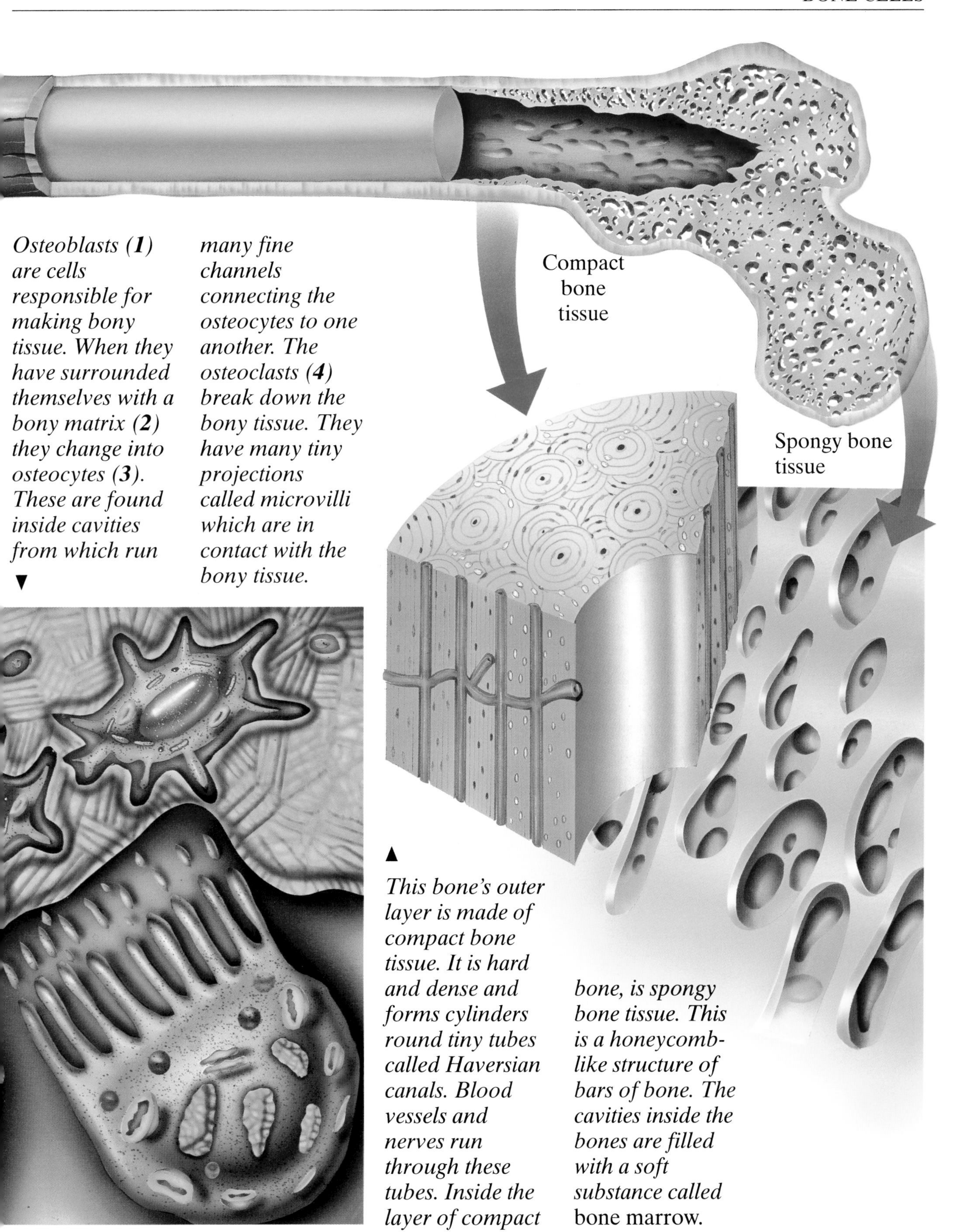

*Osteoblasts (**1**) are cells responsible for making bony tissue. When they have surrounded themselves with a bony matrix (**2**) they change into osteocytes (**3**). These are found inside cavities from which run many fine channels connecting the osteocytes to one another. The osteoclasts (**4**) break down the bony tissue. They have many tiny projections called microvilli which are in contact with the bony tissue.*

▼

▲

This bone's outer layer is made of compact bone tissue. It is hard and dense and forms cylinders round tiny tubes called Haversian canals. Blood vessels and nerves run through these tubes. Inside the layer of compact bone, is spongy bone tissue. This is a honeycomb-like structure of bars of bone. The cavities inside the bones are filled with a soft substance called bone marrow.

Surface cells and secretions

Some cells fit close together like paving stones, with no fibrous material in between. Cells like this make up the epithelial tissue that covers the various organs of the body. There are two main kinds of epithelial tissue – lining epithelium and glandular epithelium.

Lining epithelium covers and protects the external and internal surfaces of the body. There are various different types of lining epithelium. Endothelium is made up of a single layer of flat cells. It lines the inside of some organs, such as blood vessels and the stomach. On one surface they may have hairlike cilia, as in the epithelium lining the nose. Stratified epithelium is made up of several layers of flattened cells on top of one another. It forms the outer layer of the skin, the mucous membrane lining the mouth, the lining of the oesophagus and so on.

The second major kind of epithelial tissue is called glandular epithelium. It is made up of cells that manufacture and secrete one or more substances needed by the body. These substances can be for protection (gastric mucus to cover and protect the lining of the stomach from digestive juices); for digestion (enzymes of the salivary glands to begin breaking down our food); or for regulating the body (hormones to stimulate growth, perspiration to cool us down, and so on).

Glands are organs made of glandular epithelium. There are two main kinds of gland. Exocrine glands discharge their products (such as sweat) on to the surface of the body or into channels, called ducts, which carry the secretions to other parts of the body. Endocrine glands discharge their products (including hormones) directly into the blood, which carries them round the body.

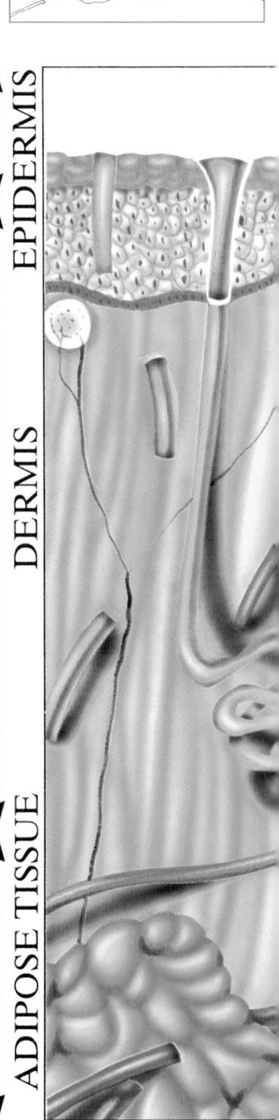

*The outer part of our skin, the epidermis, is made of stratified epithelial tissue. The deepest layers of cells in the epidermis are constantly reproducing themselves and moving towards the surface. As they do so, they produce a hard protective protein called keratin. They flatten and die, and eventually flake off as scurf. Below the epidermis is the dermis. It is made of connective tissue with elastic fibres, and contains sweat glands (**1**), hairs (**2**), and sebaceous glands (**3**). Through the dermis run blood vessels and nerve fibres, and beneath it is a layer of adipose cells which contain fat.* ►

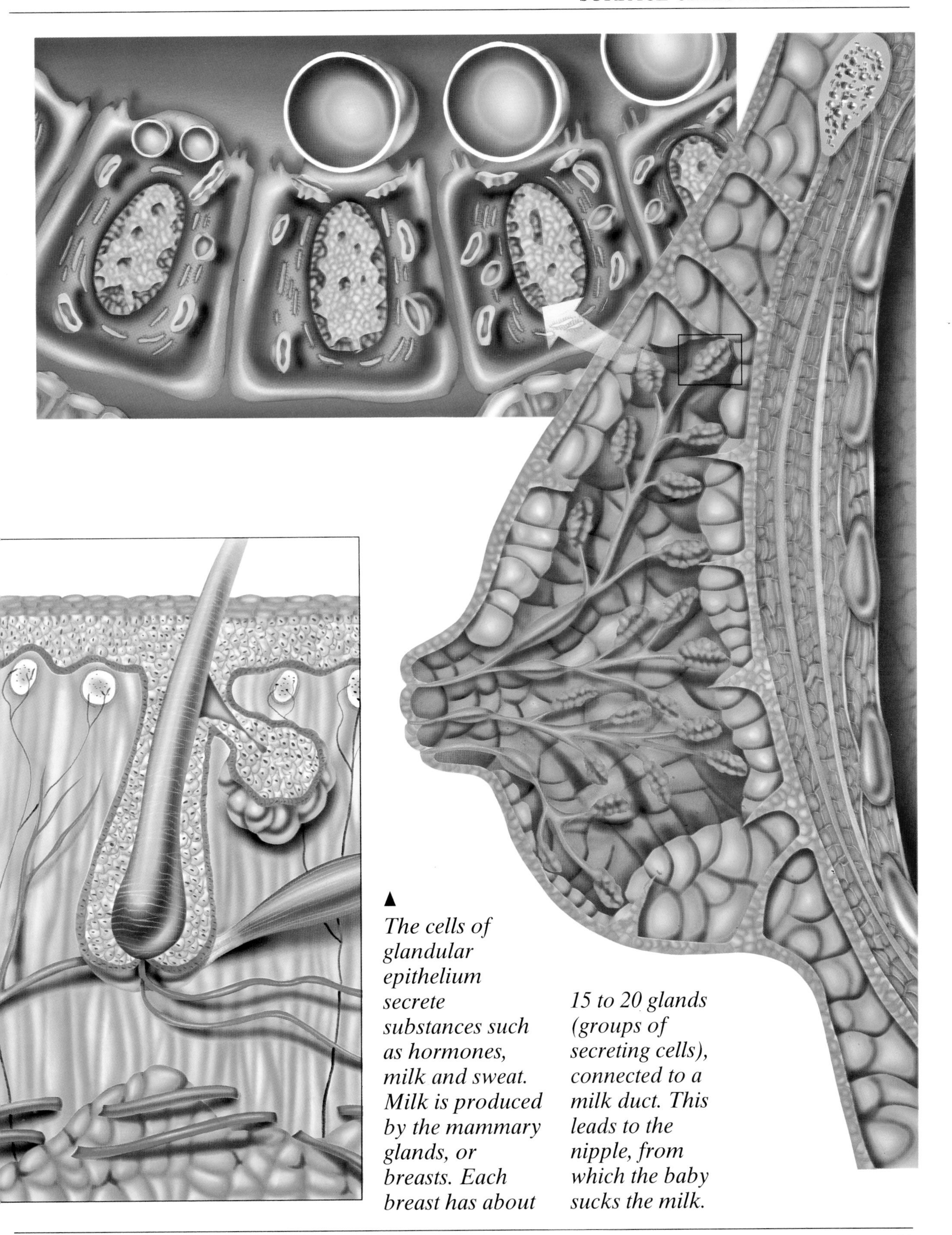

▲ *The cells of glandular epithelium secrete substances such as hormones, milk and sweat. Milk is produced by the mammary glands, or breasts. Each breast has about 15 to 20 glands (groups of secreting cells), connected to a milk duct. This leads to the nipple, from which the baby sucks the milk.*

Nerve cells

Our bodies contain many cells that take in information from stimuli outside and inside the body. They decide what, if any, action needs to be taken, and send out instructions to other parts of the body for action. These are called nerve cells, or neurons. A typical neuron consists of a cell body, containing the nucleus, and two types of extensions called *dendrites* and *axons*. Dendrites are usually short, with a wide base and treelike branches. They carry messages called nerve impulses to the cell body. Most neurons have several dendrites and a single axon. The message, or nerve impulse, is passed on from the cell body down the axon. This usually has a narrower base than a dendrite, and can be very long; an axon carrying a message from the spine right down your arm or leg can reach a metre or more in length! At its end it divides into tiny branches. Nerve impulses are passed along by a mixture of chemical and electrical activity.

Nerve cells are grouped together in bundles, simply known as nerves. They have a very long life – 100 years or more – but unlike the body's other cells, nerve cells cannot be replaced when they die.

Nerve cells do our thinking; millions of them packed together make up the brain, which acts as the central computer of the body. It interprets nerve messages, and works out what response is needed. The brain is connected to all parts of the body by a network of nerves, many of which run through the spinal cord.

Special receptor cells in our eyes, ears and other sense organs, and in our skin respond to physical stimuli such as light, sound, heat and pressure. They convert the stimuli into nerve impulses. Each kind of receptor cell is highly specialized; in the eye, for example, there are two different kinds of light-sensitive receptor cells. There are about 125 million rod cells, which are very sensitive to light but cannot distinguish colour, and 7 million cone cells which are sensitive to colour and fine detail.

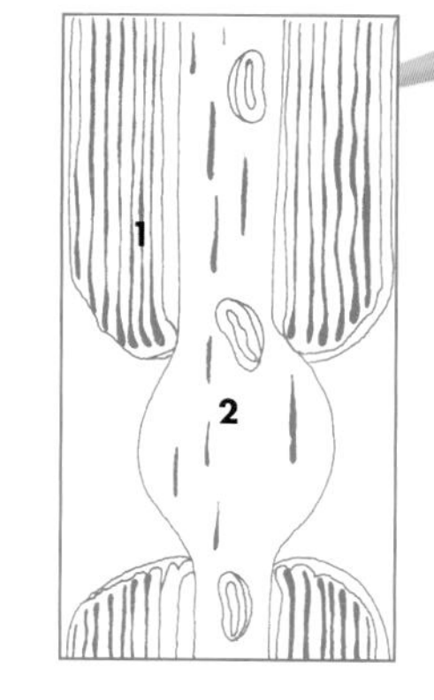

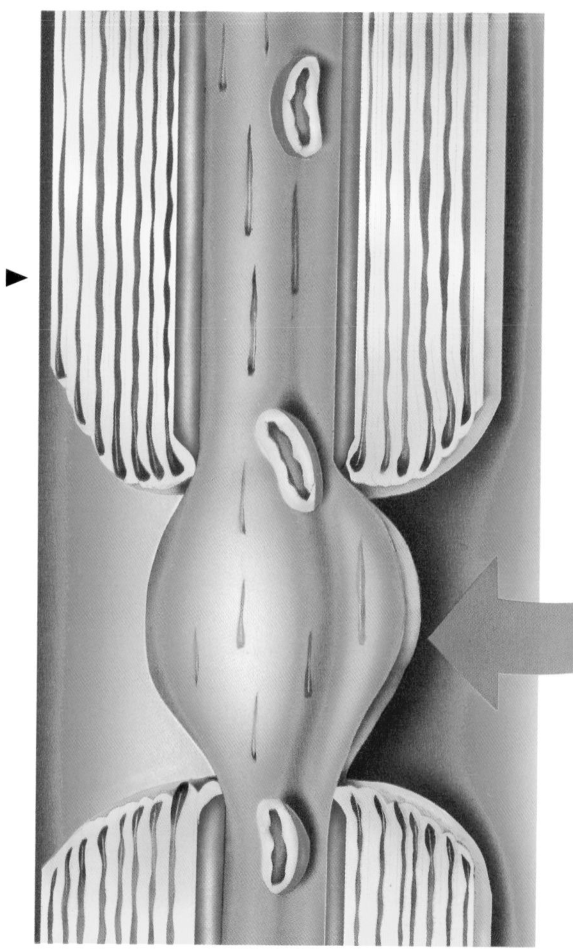

*The axons of some nerves are surrounded by a sheath of a white substance called myelin (**1**), formed by glial cells. Along the sheath are gaps called nodes of Ranvier (**2**). The nerve impulse travelling down the axon 'jumps' from one node to the next, which increases the speed of transmission.* ►

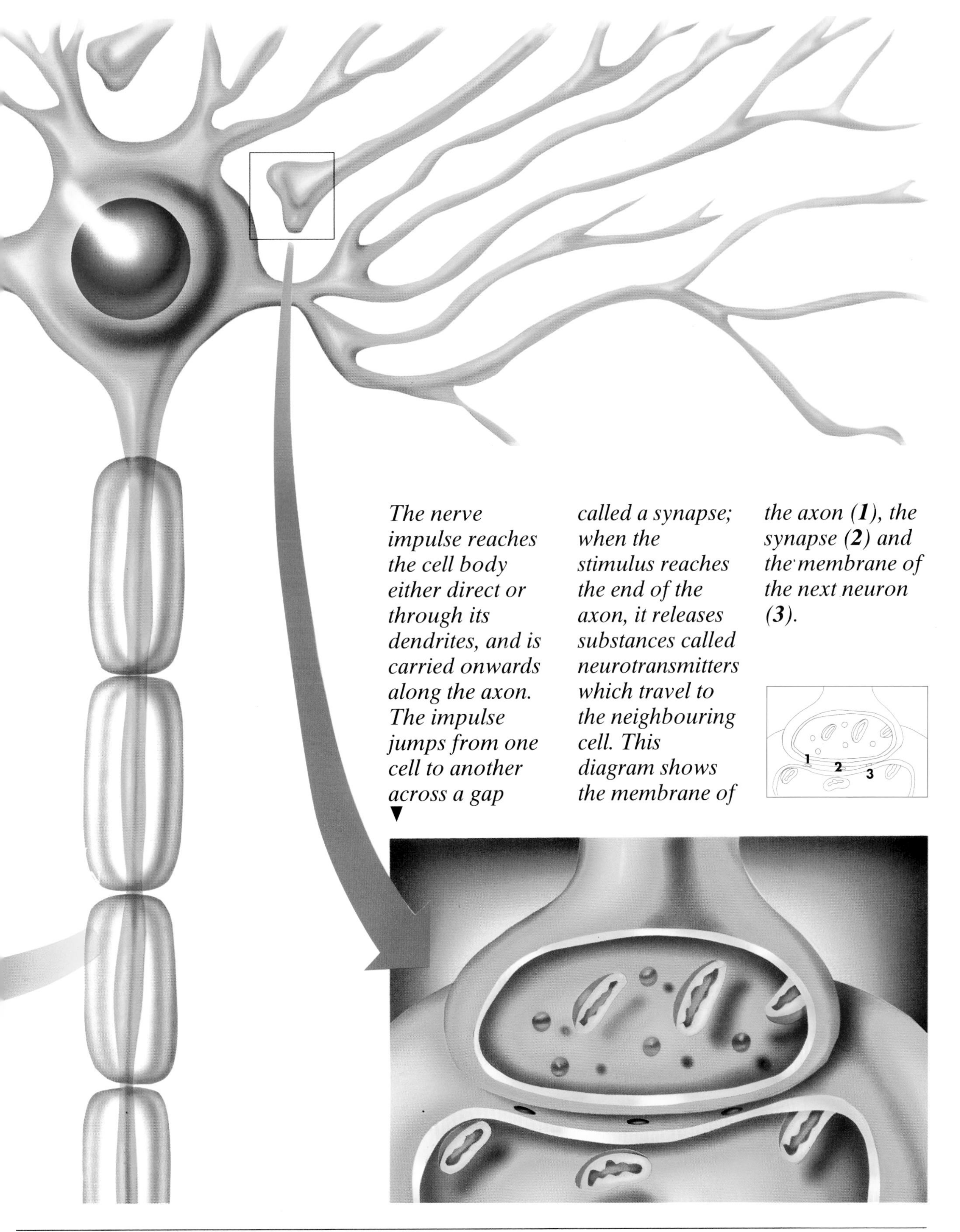

The nerve impulse reaches the cell body either direct or through its dendrites, and is carried onwards along the axon. The impulse jumps from one cell to another across a gap ▼ *called a synapse; when the stimulus reaches the end of the axon, it releases substances called neurotransmitters which travel to the neighbouring cell. This diagram shows the membrane of the axon (**1**), the synapse (**2**) and the membrane of the next neuron (**3**).*

Muscle cells

All our movements are made by muscles, bundles of long cells called fibres which contract (shorten) when they receive messages from the brain, and then relax again. Some of our movements are conscious – we can control them. The muscles that carry out these movements are called *voluntary muscles*. Other muscles keep working without our being aware of them, for example the muscles that move food along the digestive tract. These are called *involuntary muscles*. The heart is made up of a third kind of muscle, called *cardiac muscle*.

The different sorts of muscle are made up of different kinds of cell, but all muscle cells contain myofibrils (filaments) of proteins called *actin* and *myosin*.

Each long cell of voluntary muscle tissue has several nuclei. Its thick myosin filaments and thin actin filaments are arranged in regular, overlapping bands called sarcomeres. If you look at voluntary muscle tissue under a microscope, the sarcomeres show up as stripes, so voluntary muscle is also called striped muscle.

The cells of involuntary muscle tissue have one nucleus each, and are spindle shaped. They are arranged in flat sheets, and they are found in the walls of blood vessels and other hollow organs such as the stomach. Their contractions push along the contents.

Cardiac muscle has branched cells with one or two nuclei. The criss-cross arrangement of its striped fibres helps it to beat regularly and strongly for many years.

When a nerve impulse reaches the muscle, the fibres slide over one another, shortening the muscle by as much as 50 per cent. This takes a lot of energy, so muscle cells contain large numbers of mitochondria. When muscles are working hard and using energy they produce heat, so you feel warm.

The number of muscle cells in the body is always the same, but exercise increases the size of the individual cells and so the muscles grow larger and stronger.

*There are three types of muscle tissue. Voluntary muscles (**1**) are made up of striped fibres; the muscles help us move about. Cardiac muscle (**2**), which makes up the heart, has striped fibres arranged in a network. The smooth tissue of involuntary muscles (**3**) is found in blood vessels and our internal organs. We have no conscious control over these muscles.*

▼

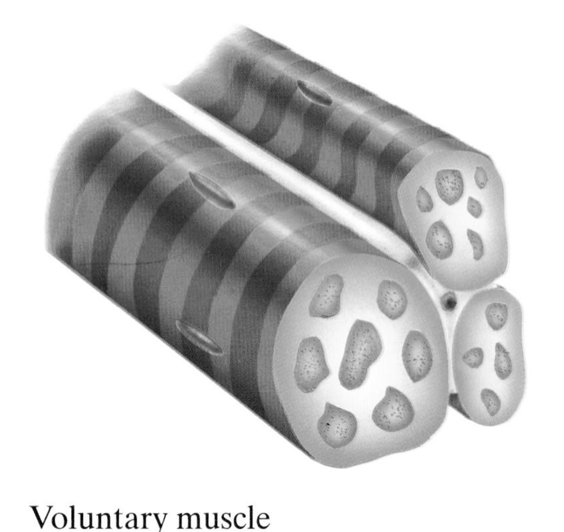

Voluntary muscle (Striped fibres)

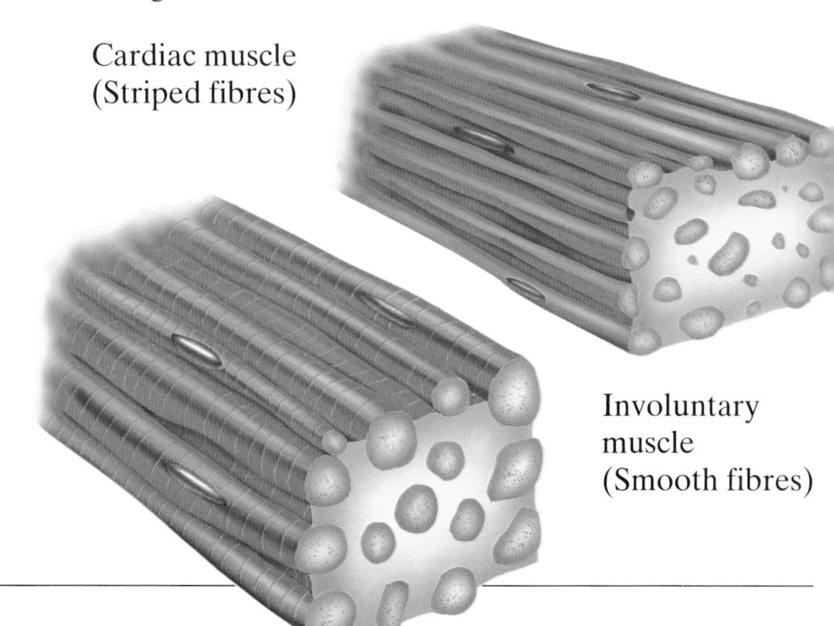

Cardiac muscle (Striped fibres)

Involuntary muscle (Smooth fibres)

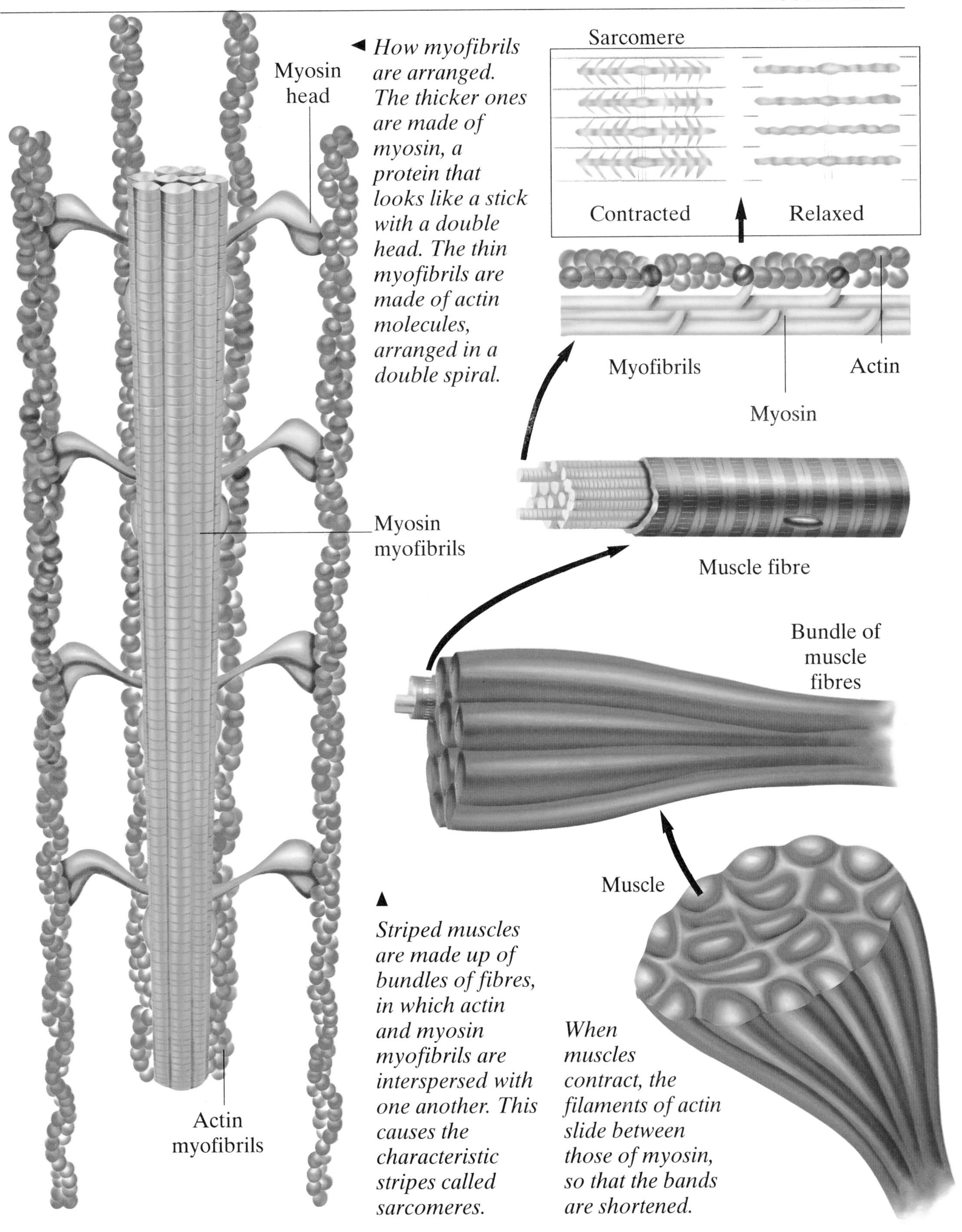

◄ *How myofibrils are arranged. The thicker ones are made of myosin, a protein that looks like a stick with a double head. The thin myofibrils are made of actin molecules, arranged in a double spiral.*

▲ *Striped muscles are made up of bundles of fibres, in which actin and myosin myofibrils are interspersed with one another. This causes the characteristic stripes called sarcomeres.*

When muscles contract, the filaments of actin slide between those of myosin, so that the bands are shortened.

Blood cells

Our cells need a supply of oxygen and nutrients; they must get rid of waste products; and the substances they make need to be taken round the body to other cells. Cells that defend the body from infections must be able to move around. These needs are met by the blood in the network of tubes that circulates it round the body.

Blood is a red, sticky liquid. It is made up of a clear, yellowish fluid called *plasma* which contains several different kinds of cells – *red blood cells*, or erythrocytes, white blood cells, or leucocytes, and *platelets*, or thrombocytes. Red and white cells are sometimes called corpuscles. The plasma also carries round nutrients from digested food, water, waste products and substances manufactured and sent out by the cells.

Oxygen is carried in the blood by the red cells. These contain a protein called haemoglobin, which combines easily with oxygen from the air as it passes through the lungs. They release it to the cells. A red blood cell lives for about four months, during which time it travels about 480 kilometres through the human body! It has no nucleus, which means that it does not use up much energy or many materials. It is a tiny flattened disc with a very flexible membrane so that it can bend to pass through very narrow blood vessels. Each millilitre of blood contains between 4,000 and 5,000 million red blood cells.

The white blood cells play an important part in defending the body. These cells are larger than the red cells, and there is only one white cell to every 700 red cells. Some white cells, called lymphocytes, produce antibodies, defence proteins which attack foreign substances entering the body. They have many ribosomes to make these proteins. Other white cells, such as granulocytes and monocytes, destroy germs by engulfing them and then digesting them. Platelets are fragments of larger cells which play an important part in the *clotting* (coagulation) of the blood by making chemicals called tissue-clotting factors. If the blood did not clot when we cut ourselves, we should go on bleeding.

Red and white blood cells are made by 'mother' cells in the bone marrow, a jellylike substance found in the body's largest bones. Lymphocytes are also made in the lymph glands. Mother cells may change, grow large and break into fragments; these are the platelets.

Blood is made up of a liquid called plasma which carries different types of cells with different functions. Red blood cells are flattish disc-shaped cells that carry oxygen to all the cells in the body. They give blood its red colour. White cells defend the body against invading organisms such as bacteria. Platelets play a part in the clotting of blood. ►

White cells are made in the bone marrow from cells called myeloblasts, lymphoblasts and monoblasts. Lymphocytes are

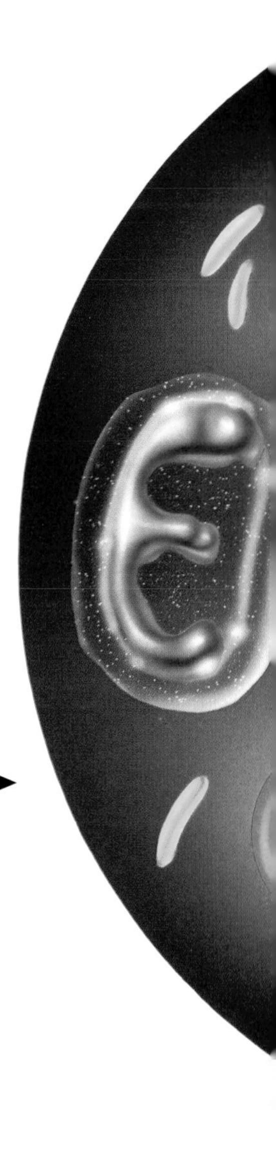

also made in lymph glands. Monocytes can leave the blood vessels and turn themselves into macrophages which destroy bacteria. ►

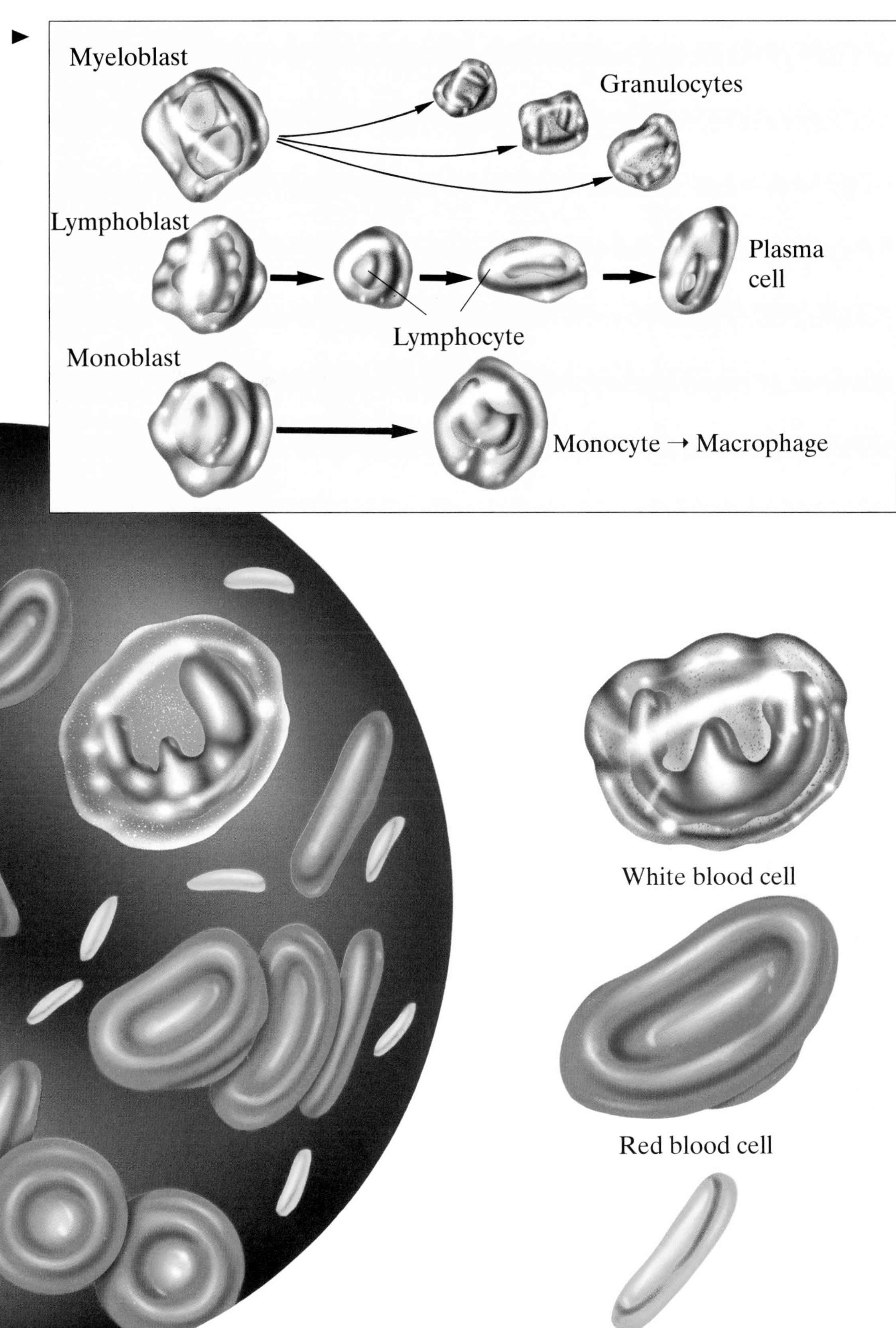

Finding out

How to look at cells

Almost all cells are so small that we cannot see them without the aid of a microscope. This is an instrument containing a series of lenses that greatly enlarge anything seen through them. For us to see cells under a microscope, they first need to be spread out on a small rectangle of glass called a slide. To make them clearer, they can be stained with dye. The slide is placed on the microscope's platform, and a bright light is shone through the slide from beneath. When you look through the eyepiece of the microscope, you can focus the lens on the slide. Using a microscope is very easy after a little practice.

A small microscope like this has several lenses that magnify tiny cells. Larger microscopes can make cells appear millions of times larger. ▼

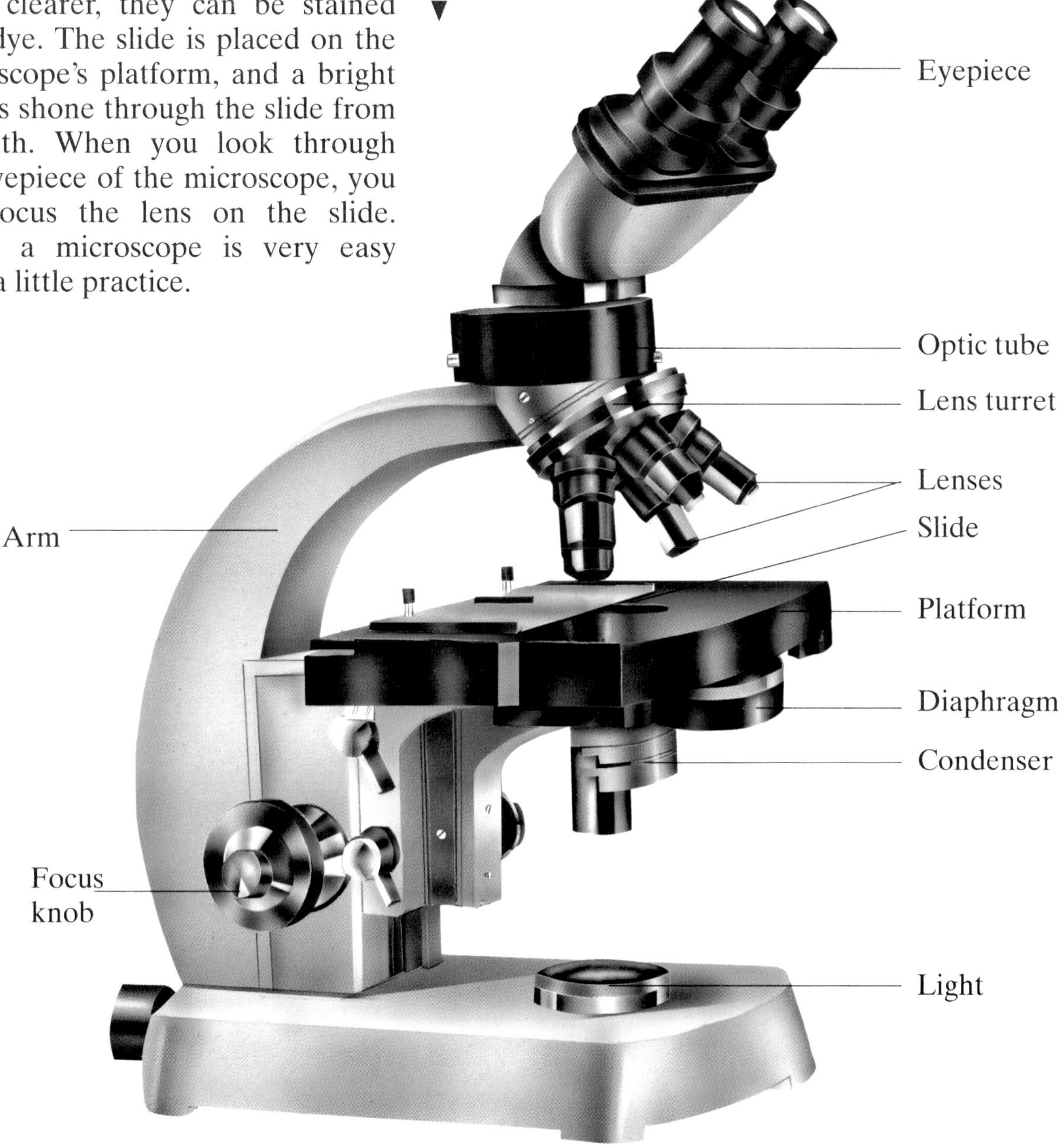

Looking at your own cells

You can look at some of your own cells in this experiment. You need a slide, a slide cover, and some blue methylene dye. First, gently scrape along the inside of your cheek with a clean spatula or fingernail. Smear the liquid you collect on the slide to make a thin film. If you looked at the cells now, they would appear almost transparent and you would see very little. To avoid this, put a drop of blue methylene dye on the slide. Leave it for three or four minutes, and then rinse the slide with water. The dye will have stained the cells so that you can see their different parts clearly. Put the slide cover over the cells and put the slide on the microscope platform. You should be able to make out some cells with their outer membranes, their nuclei and a number of spots, which are the organelles of the cells' cytoplasm. You are looking at lining epithelial cells.

The cells from the lining tissue of your cheeks are easy to scrape off and smear on a slide with a spatula. ▼

Spread them as thin as possible to prevent them overlapping and obscuring each other.

Your blood under the microscope
If you want to, you can look at your blood cells. Get a sterile needle, and carefully clean and disinfect your fingertip. Prick it with the needle, and squeeze a drop of blood on to a slide. Spread it out well. Put on the slide cover, and place it under the microscope. You will be able to see some of your red blood cells. The white ones will be transparent; if you want to see them, you need a special stain. If you are doing this experiment with someone else, make sure you do not under any circumstances use the same needle. Diseases can be transmitted by the blood.

Never use the same needle as someone else when you do this experiment. Put a drop of blood on the slide, and then smear it thinly with the help of another slide. Wash the slide afterwards.

Index and glossary

A
Actin 24, 25
A protein found in muscle fibre filaments.
Adipose cells/tissue 18, 20
Amino acids 5, 6
The building blocks of proteins. Some can be manufactured by our bodies but eight vital amino acids can only be provided by the proteins in our food.
Ammonia 5
A colourless gas.
Amoeba 4
A single-celled animal that moves by means of pseudopods.
Anabolism 10
The metabolic process in which simple molecules form more complex molecules and energy is taken up and stored.
Atmosphere, earth's 4
Autophagy 10, 11
Axons 22, 23
Long nerve fibres, one coming from each neuron, that transmit nerve impulses.

B
Bacteria 4, 8, 10, 12, 27
Micro-organisms, many of which cause infections or diseases when they enter the blood.
Bases, chemical 7
Blastula 17
Blood 10, 20, 26, 27, 29
Blood vessels 13, 20, 24, 26, 27, 29
The arteries, arterioles, capillaries and veins which carry blood all round the body.
Bone, bony tissue 14, 16, 18, 19
Bone marrow 19, 26
Soft tissue found in some bones. Red marrow is a spongy red substance which produces blood cells; yellow marrow is a fat store.
Brain 12, 22, 24
A large mass of soft nerve tissue within the skull that controls almost all our bodily functions.
Breast 21

C
Calcium 6, 18
Carbohydrates 6, 9
Substances obtained from our food that are converted into glucose, which supplies our cells with energy.
Carbon 4, 6
A chemical element found in all organic compounds.
Carbon dioxide 11, 16, 26
A gas that forms as a waste product during the body's processes, and is carried by the blood to the lungs, from where it is breathed out.
Cardiac muscle 24
The special muscle tissue from which the heart is formed.
Cartilage, cartilaginous tissue 16, 18
Tough, flexible material that makes up part of the skeleton and also the ear flap and part of the nose.
Catabolism 10
The metabolic process in which substances are broken down with the release of energy.
Cell membrane *see* Membrane, cell
Cellular nutrition 10
Cellular sensitivity 12
Centrioles 14
Chondrocytes 18
Chromatid 14
A copy of a chromosome formed during cell division.
Chromosomes 14, 15
Threadlike structures containing DNA, found in the nucleus of a cell. They carry the genes inherited from our parents.
Cilia 12, 20
Tiny hairlike projections from the outer surface of some cells, which wave to and fro to move liquids and other substances around them.
Clotting 26
The process in which blood thickens to form a jellylike mass or clot.
Collagen 16, 18
Connective tissue 16, 18
Cytoplasm 8, 9, 10, 12, 18, 29
The contents of the cell (excluding the nucleus), including a watery substance containing a mixture of particles and dissolved chemicals and a number of structures called organelles. These carry out the cell's functions, producing energy, building proteins, and so on.

D
Dendrites 22
Short nerve fibres, often several to a neuron, that pick up nerve impulses from other neurons.
Deoxyribonucleic acid *see* DNA
Dermis 20
Digestion 6, 10, 20
The process by which our food is broken down into nutrients that can be absorbed and used by the body's cells.
Digestive juices 16, 20
Division, cellular 14-17
DNA (deoxyribonucleic acid) 6-9, 14
The substance contained in the cell nucleus which is inherited from our parents and which carries coded instructions for all cell processes in the form of genes.
Ducts 20, 21

E
Earth, primitive 4
Elastin 16, 18
Embryo 16
An organism in the earliest stages of its development.
Endoplasmic reticulum 8
Endocrine glands 20
Endothelium 20
Energy 6, 8, 10, 11, 24
Enzymes 8, 10, 20
Protein products of our cells

that take part in chemical changes in the body while remaining unchanged themselves.
Epidermis 20
Epithelial tissue (epithelium) 16, 20, 21, 29
Erythrocytes *see* Red blood cells
Eukaryotic cells 9
Exocrine glands 20, 21
Exocytosis 10
The process in which substances made in the cell pass through its membrane.
Eye 22

F
Fats 6, 8, 9, 18 *see also* Lipids
Fibroblasts 16, 18
Flagella 12, 13
Food 10, 20, 26

G
Gases 4
Gastrulation 17
Genes 6, 8, 14
The basic units, formed from DNA, that carry inherited, or genetic, characteristics.
Genetic material 6, 9, 14, 16
Glands 20
Organs or structures in the body that produce useful substances, such as hormones and digestive juices, or that separate unwanted substances from the blood and dispose of them.
Glandular epithelium 20, 21
Glial cells 22
Glucose 6, 7, 8, 11
A form of sugar produced by the breaking down of carbohydrates in our food, which supplies energy to the body.
Glycogen 6, 7
The form in which glucose is stored in the liver and muscles. When energy is needed, glycogen is quickly converted back into glucose.
Golgi apparatus 8
Granulocytes 11, 26, 27

H
Haemoglobin 26
Hairs 20
Haversian canals 19
Heart 16, 20, 24
Hereditary material *see* Genetic material
Heterophagy 10, 11
Hormones 8, 10, 20, 21
Chemicals, produced by glands and specialized cells in the body, which control body processes. They are carried round in the blood.
Hydrogen 4, 5, 6
A gas found in air, water and all living things.

I
Infections 12, 13, 26
Invertebrate animals 10
Animals without backbones.
Involuntary muscles 24
Muscles made up of smooth fibres, not under our conscious control; also called smooth muscles.

K
Keratin 20
Kidneys 18

L
Leucocytes *see* White blood cells
Ligaments 18
Lining tissue *see* Epithelial tissue
Lipids 6, 8, 9
Fats and oils processed from our foods and used in our cells as fuel. They are stored in the body as a reserve supply of energy. They are major components of the cell membrane.
Liver 16
Lungs 10, 16
Lymphoblasts 26, 27
Lymphocytes 26, 27
Lysosomes 8, 10

M
Macrophage 27
Mammary glands 21
Marrow, bone 19, 26, 27
Matrix, bone 18, 19
Meiosis 14, 15
The special process of cell division which results in the formation of reproductive cells with half the normal number of chromosomes.
Membrane, cell 6, 8, 9, 10, 12, 16, 23, 26
The thin layer of lipids and proteins that surrounds and contains the cytoplasm of the cell.
Membrane, nuclear 14
Metabolism 8, 10
The complex processes that transform substances in the cell into energy and useful products, and dispose of waste products.
Methane 5
A gas formed when living things decay.
Micro-organisms 13
Microscope 4, 24, 28, 29
Microvilli 16, 19
Tiny fingerlike projections of the cell membrane and cytoplasm.
Milk 21
Miller, Stanley 5
Mitochondria 8, 10, 11, 24
Mitosis 14
The process in which a cell divides into two exact replicas of itself, each containing identical chromosomes.
Molecule 4, 5, 6, 7, 9, 10
The smallest particle of a substance.
Monocytes 10, 27
Morula 17
Mouth 20
Movements of body 24
Movements of cells 12
Mucous membrane 12
Mucus 12, 16, 20
Slimy substance secreted by mucous membrane.
Muscle cells/fibres/tissue 16, 18, 24, 25 *see also* Involuntary muscles; Voluntary muscles
Myelin 22
Myeloblasts 26, 27
Myofibrils 24, 25
Myosin 24, 25
A protein found in the muscle fibre.

N
Nerve cells (fibres) 12, 16, 18, 20, 22, 23
Nerve impulses 22, 23, 24
Nerve tissue 16, 22
Neurons *see* Nerve cells.
Nitrogen 4, 6
A gas that makes up about 78 per cent of the air.
Nucleic acids 5, 6
Substance that carries our

genetic material; it is made of sugar, phosphoric acid and the bases adenine, cytosine, guanine and thymine arranged in spiralling bands. See also DNA *and* RNA.
Nucleus 8, 9, 14, 22, 24, 26
The central part of the cell, surrounded by its own membrane, that contains the chromosomes.
Nutrients 8, 10, 26
Substances derived from food that are used to build new cells and tissues or are used to provide the cells with energy.

O
Oesophagus 20
Oparin, Alexander Ivanovich 4
Organelles 5, 8, 9, 10, 11, 18
Structures within the cytoplasm of the cell, including ribosomes, the endoplasmic reticulum, the Golgi apparatus, lysosomes and mitochondria. Each has a specific function to perform, such as producing energy, breaking down molecules, building proteins, and so on.
Organic compounds (molecules) 4, 5, 6
Groups of chemicals that contain carbon from which all living matter is formed
Organs 16, 18, 20
Ossification 18
Osteoblasts 18, 19
Osteoclasts 18. 19
Osteocytes 18, 19
Ovaries 14
Ovum 12-15, 17
Female sex cell, or egg.
Oxygen 4, 6, 8, 10, 11, 16, 26
A gas, essential to life, which is absorbed through the lungs and carried by the blood to all the body's tissues, where it is used to 'burn' food to release energy.

P
Peptides 12
Perspiration 20
Phagocytosis 10-12, 27
The process in which cells surround and take in larger molecules and particles, for example when white blood cells surround and digest foreign substances such as bacteria.
Phosphorus 6
Plasma 26
The watery liquid part of the blood, in which blood cells, nutrients, antibodies, hormones, waste products and other substances are carried round the body.
Platelets 26, 27
Small oval cells carried in the blood which produce blood-clotting factors. They are also called thrombocytes.
Polar bodies 15
Primeval soup 4
Prokaryotic cells 9
Proteins 5, 6, 8, 9, 16, 18, 20, 24, 25
Substances obtained from our food that are essential for the body's growth and maintenance.
Pseudopods 12, 13

R
Ranvier, nodes of 22
Receptor cells 12, 22
Receptor molecules 8
Substances in the cell wall that detect changes in the cell's environment.
Red blood cells 26, 27
Disc-shaped cells in the blood, produced in the red bone marrow, containing the pigment haemoglobin. They pick up oxygen in the lungs and carry it round the body. They are also called erythrocytes.
Reproduction 10
Respiratory system 16
Ribonucleic acid *see* RNA
Ribosomes 8, 16, 27
RNA (Ribonucleic acid) 6, 8
Nucleic acid involved in the manufacture of proteins.

S
Salivary glands 20
Sarcomeres 24, 25
Secretory cells 20, 21
Sense organs 12
Sensory cells *see* Receptor cells
Sex cells 12, 14
Single-celled organisms 4, 10
Skin 14, 20, 22
Spermatozoa (sperm) 12-15, 17
Male sex cells.
Spinal cord 22
Stimuli 12, 22, 23
Stomach 14, 16, 20, 24
Striped muscles *see* Voluntary muscles,
Sweat 20
Synapse 23
System 16
Several organs working together to carry out a specific function, for example the digestive system, circulatory system and respiratory system, each of which contains several organs made up of different kinds of tissue.

T
Tendons 18
Testicles 14
Thrombocytes *see* Platelets
Tissues 16, 18
Collections of specialized cells or fibres carrying out particular jobs or forming particular structures, such as bones.

V
Vesicle 10
Voluntary muscles 24, 25
Muscles, made up of striated (striped) fibres, that can be consciously controlled; also known as striped muscles.

W
Water 4-6, 26
White blood cells 10, 12, 13, 26, 27
Large cells that form part of the body's defence system, and are carried in the blood to wherever they are needed. They are also called leucocytes. Most white blood cells are made in the red bone marrow but some, called, lymphocytes, are also made in the lymph glands.

Z
Zygote 14, 16, 17
The cell formed when a sperm and ovum unite.